MARRIAGE ON THE ROCK

25ᵀᴴ ANNIVERSARY EDITION

JIMMY EVANS

Marriage on the Rock Study Guide
Copyright © 2024 by Jimmy Evans

All Scripture quotations, unless otherwise indicated, are taken from the *Holy Bible*, New International Version®, NIV®. Copyright ©1973, 1978, 1984, 2011 by Biblica, Inc.™ Used by permission of Zondervan. All rights reserved worldwide. www.zondervan.com. The "NIV" and "New International Version" are trademarks registered in the United States Patent and Trademark Office by Biblica, Inc.™

Scripture quotations marked (KJV) are taken from the King James Version of the Bible. Public domain.

Scripture quotations marked (NASB) are taken from the (NASB®) New American Standard Bible®, Copyright © 1960, 1971, 1977, 1995, 2020 by The Lockman Foundation. Used by permission. All rights reserved. lockman.org.

Scripture quotations marked (NKJV) are taken from the New King James Version®. Copyright © 1982 by Thomas Nelson. Used by permission. All rights reserved.

Scripture quotations marked (NLT) are taken from the *Holy Bible*, New Living Translation, copyright ©1996, 2004, 2015 by Tyndale House Foundation. Used by permission of Tyndale House Publishers, Carol Stream, Illinois 60188. All rights reserved.

All rights reserved. No portion of this publication may be reproduced, stored in a retrieval system, or transmitted in any form by any means—electronic, mechanical, photocopying, recording, or any other—without prior permission from the publisher. "XO Marriage" is a trademark registered in the United States Patent and Trademark Office by XO Marriage.

ISBN: 978-1-960870-22-3

XO Publishing is a leading creator of relationship-based resources. We focus primarily on marriage-related content for churches, small group curriculum, and people looking for timeless truths about relationships and overall marital health. For more information on other resources from XO Publishing, visit XOPublishing.com.

XO Marriage®, an imprint of XO Publishing
1021 Grace Lane
Southlake, Texas 76092

Printed in the United States of America
24 25 26 27—5 4 3 2 1

Table of Contents

Introduction v

Leader Guide ix

1. Finding the Rock 1
2. The Four Foundational Laws of Marriage 9
3. The Law of Priority 15
4. The Law of Pursuit 23
5. The Law of Possession 31
6. The Law of Purity 37
7. God's Blueprint for Marital Bliss 45
8 & 9. The Destructive Husband &
  Four Kinds of Destructive Husbands 53
10. How to Understand and Meet Your
   Wife's Needs 63
11 & 12. The Destructive Wife & Four Kinds
   of Destructive Wives 71
13. How to Understand and Meet Your
   Husband's Needs 79

14 & 15. When You Are Building Alone &
   Four Principles for Building Alone 87

16. Sweet and Sour Pleasure 95

17. Skills for Communication 101

18. Skills for Financial Success 109

19. Skills for Successful Parenting 119

20. Skills for Sexual Pleasure 129

21. Skills for In-Law Relations 137

22. Skills for Remarriage and Blended
    Families 147

Notes 159

Introduction

Welcome to the *Marriage on the Rock Study Guide*! I created this study guide as a companion resource to *Marriage on the Rock*, and you will notice that it follows the same section and chapter order. The purpose of this study guide is to help you dive even deeper into the book's material so that you can incorporate the principles into your own life and marriage. You can use it for yourself, or better yet, read it together with your spouse. This study guide is also a helpful tool for leaders of small groups and marriage classes.

Here is the layout for each chapter in this study guide:

The Big Idea
This brief section presents the primary theme, thought, or truth from the chapter.

Review
The review summarizes the chapter's content and highlights important insights and details. It serves as a refresher if you have finished the chapter some

days before you get to the discussion and reflection questions. The review can also be read aloud if you are going through the book with your spouse or with a small group or class.

Scripture Reading

I encourage you to read these Scriptures carefully and meditate on them throughout the day. What is the Holy Spirit saying to you through God's Word? Be sure to write down what you hear in your heart.

Discussion Questions

The discussion questions prompt you to recall important concepts or to think through particular applications. They are great discussion starters for couples, small groups, and classes. Individuals can also find it helpful to write down their answers in a journal.

Reflection Questions

The reflection questions are more personal in nature and focus on your own relationship and experiences. They are best suited for personal and couple responses. This is another opportunity to journal your answers and let the Holy Spirit guide you in growing together. Even if you are doing this study guide alone, I encourage you to share your answers with your spouse. The best way to build your marriage is to build it *with* your spouse!

Connect with God

This sample prayer offers a conversation-starter with God about the things you have read and reflected on in the chapter. You can pray the prayer aloud by yourself, with your spouse, or with your group or class. But don't stop there! Ask the Holy Spirit to continue speaking to you and guiding you as you grow in your relationship with the Lord and with your spouse.

Leader Guide

Whether this is your first time to lead a book study or you have a lot of leadership experience, I am confident that God is going to use you in a powerful way. Lasting marriages are built on a foundation of love expressed through honesty, vulnerability, trust, and selflessness. You are partnering with God in providing opportunities for that to happen, and I am so thankful for you.

I've included a sample 60-minute session schedule to help you structure your time together. I've also listed some guidance on how to prepare for and lead these sessions. The best leader is, of course, the Holy Spirit. Always seek His guidance and listen to His direction. And if you need to make some adjustments and changes for your group or class, feel free to do so. The Holy Spirit's plan is always the best one!

Sample Session Schedule

Welcome: 5 minutes
Read ("Big Idea," "Review," and "Scripture Reading"): 20 minutes
Discussion Questions: 25 minutes
Prayer ("Connect with God"): 10 minutes

Before the Session

Pray

Prayer is the most important thing you can do to prepare. We all need God's help, and He is more than willing to come to our assistance if we will simply ask Him. Here are some prayer points you might consider:

- Pray for each person's relationship with the Lord.
- Pray for each person's relationship with their spouse.
- Pray for each person's relationship with their children.
- Pray for the Holy Spirit to give you wisdom.

Prepare

Read the chapter in the book and in this study guide that you will be discussing in your next session. As you read, make notes of anything that stands out to you. These can be quotes from the text, Scripture passages, stories, ideas, and so forth. Next, review the discussion and personal reflection questions and mentally answer them for yourself. This will help you become more familiar with the material and build your confidence.

Plan Ahead

Assign a backup leader who will be prepared to lead the session if an emergency arises and you are unable to attend. Also, if you need to make a schedule change, do your best to communicate with the group members in advance. By keeping the lines of communication open, you build trust and cooperation.

During the Session

Be Punctual

Few things convey indifference as strongly as a leader who doesn't manage their time well. Yes, life can get in the way of the best intentions, but strive to arrive on time, or even early, for every session. Begin promptly and end on time. This demonstrates your respect for the time of everyone in your group.

Be Engaged

The people in your small group will reflect your level of engagement. In other words, the more engaged you are, the more they will be too. Do your best to be 100 percent present and make a conscious effort to eliminate distractions. This includes turning off your cell phone, or at least setting it on "silent" or "do not disturb" mode. Invite the group members to do the same.

Be Trustworthy

During the first session, set an expectation of safety and discretion. Tell your group that everything shared within the sessions should remain confidential within the group. This will help the group members feel more at ease, particularly during the discussion times. It may take a few moments for conversation to pick up, and that's perfectly fine. Remember, you do not have to "teach" these chapters. Your responsibility is to set the stage for conversations, and the Holy Spirit will begin to move as people share their thoughts and feelings.

Be Compassionate

Every marriage experiences its share of ups and downs. Even if members of your small group choose not to disclose the specifics, they may be facing their own challenges. There may be occasions when someone appears disengaged and reserved, or they might exhibit strong emotions during the conversation. These moments provide an opportunity to reflect the compassionate nature of our heavenly Father. As Psalm 86:15 states, "But you, O Lord, are a God of compassion and mercy, slow to get angry and filled with unfailing love and faithfulness." Allow the Holy Spirit to guide your words, actions, and demeanor, granting you wisdom in your interactions with everyone in your small group.

Additionally, remember to extend compassion to yourself. There may be times when you feel inadequate or unprepared. Always bear in mind that there is only one perfect Leader: the King of kings and Lord of lords. Keep your focus on Jesus. As Proverbs 3:6 reminds us, "Seek his will in all you do, and he will show you which path to take."

Be Calm

There will be unexpected situations and dynamics in a small group. As the leader, it is important for you to project a calm demeanor. Sometimes you may have individuals or couples who tend to dominate the discussion or want to tell everyone what to do. In those situations, gently thank them for their input and invite others to speak. If necessary, feel free to talk with them outside of the session to ask them to help you create a hospitable environment that invites everyone to participate. Sometimes, simply asking someone for their help gives them a sense of responsibility, which can improve future sessions.

As you begin, I encourage you to remind yourself that the Lord will be alongside you every step of the way. He cares even more about the couples in your group or class than you do! You don't have to do this in your own strength. God will give you everything you need as you trust Him to lead through you.

1

Finding the Rock

THE BIG IDEA

Only Jesus Christ can truly meet our deepest needs for acceptance, identity, security, and purpose. When we look to other people or things to meet these needs, we will always be disappointed.

REVIEW

Who meets your deepest needs? On a daily basis, whom do you rely on the most, and to whom do you go first? We all have physical needs, such as food, oxygen, and sleep, but there are deeper needs that relate to our heart and soul. Every human is instinctively motivated to meet these four needs:

1. **Acceptance**: Knowing you are loved and needed by others.
2. **Identity**: Knowing you are individually significant and special.

3. **Security**: Knowing you are well protected and provided for.
4. **Purpose**: Knowing you have a reason for living.

Do you know how those needs are met? Many people look to friends, family, experiences, careers, or material wealth and possessions. But even those closest to us, such as our spouse and children, cannot meet these needs. Only Jesus can. When God created human beings in His image, He built a "Jesus-sized" hole in us, and nothing and no one on earth can fill it except Jesus. Our needs are designed to draw us to Him.

The encounter between Jesus and the Samaritan woman at the well illustrates this truth. The woman had been married five times and was living with a man outside of wedlock. She was at the well alone because she was an outcast in her community and no respectful woman would be seen with her. She came to the well to meet her need for water, but Jesus spoke to her about her "soul thirst." The Samaritan woman made a mistake many of us make. She tried to get men to satisfy her soul thirst, and when they couldn't, she rejected them—thinking there must have been something wrong with them. Finally, after five failed marriages and a broken heart and shattered dreams, she gave up.

Jesus helped her to recognize that the problem wasn't with the men in her past or even herself. The problem was that she was turning to the wrong source to get her deepest needs met. All of us are soul thirsty, and only God can quench our thirst.

The first thing you need to understand for your marriage to work is that no human being can meet your deepest needs. Only God can. Your spouse can encourage you and help you experience love in a real way, but even the most spiritual person on earth is still limited. When you put too much hope in a person, you are headed for disappointment (and sometimes disaster).

When a Christian does not look to God to meet their deepest needs, they automatically transfer these expectations to the person closest to them, which is generally their spouse. This shift creates three significant problems:

1. **Perpetual Disappointment**: Regardless of how well things go in the relationship, you will always be disappointed by human limitations.
2. **Lack of Inner Resources**: Relying on others to fulfill your needs makes you dependent on their actions, hindering your ability to love them and confront life's challenges effectively.
3. **Hurt and Offense**: Trusting someone to meet your deepest needs sets you up for eventual

hurt and offense because no one can fully meet those expectations.

Sometimes the reaction to these problems is a manageable sense of frustration, but more often, it is destructive anger.

Look at the difference between when you put your trust in people and things versus putting your trust in God.

When you trust in people or things:

- Your inner security depends on unpredictable and uncontrollable factors with limited resources.
- Your ability to give is dependent upon your ability to get from others.
- Your life is filled with an atmosphere of disappointment and frustration.
- Your unrealistic expectations of others create an atmosphere of tension that drives people away.

When you trust in God:

- Your inner security and strength rest in His unwavering faithfulness and boundless resources.
- Your ability to give flows from the ever-present Holy Spirit who is within you. This allows you

to love generously even when others don't reciprocate.
- Your life is filled with an atmosphere of blessing, satisfaction, and optimism.
- Your realistic expectations of others draw you closer together as you love and give to them.

When you put your trust in Jesus, He truly satisfies your needs, transforming your life and strengthening your marriage. Jesus loves you, and He is the best friend you will ever have. As you pray and read the Word of God daily, you will experience the reality of His presence in your life.

If you will transfer your expectations to Jesus, you will not be disappointed. He is *always* faithful, and He loves you more than you love yourself or anyone else. He wants to meet your needs more than you want them met. Only a person who trusts in Jesus to this depth can truly have a successful marriage. Once Jesus is working in your life, then everything else can work.

SCRIPTURE READING

> They all ate the same spiritual food and drank the same spiritual drink; for they drank from the spiritual rock that accompanied them, and that rock was Christ (1 Corinthians 10:3–4).

> "For the bread of God is the bread that comes down from heaven and gives life to the world."

"Sir," they said, "always give us this bread."

Then Jesus declared, "I am the bread of life. Whoever comes to me will never go hungry, and whoever believes in me will never be thirsty" (John 6:33–35).

On the last and greatest day of the festival, Jesus stood and said in a loud voice, "Let anyone who is thirsty come to me and drink. Whoever believes in me, as Scripture has said, rivers of living water will flow from within them." By this he meant the Spirit, whom those who believed in him were later to receive. Up to that time the Spirit had not been given, since Jesus had not yet been glorified (John 7:37–39).

DISCUSSION QUESTIONS

1. Why is it crucial to understand who or what meets your deepest needs? How can this knowledge impact the dynamics of your relationship with your spouse?
2. The four basic needs are acceptance, identity, security, and purpose. How have you seen people try to meet these needs apart from God?
3. How does the encounter between Jesus and the Samaritan woman at the well illustrate the idea that only God can quench our soul thirst and fill the "Jesus-sized" hole?

4. What are some common consequences of misplaced trust?
5. How can transferring your expectations to Jesus lead to a more fulfilling life and marriage?

REFLECTION QUESTIONS

1. Who or what do you typically rely on to meet your deepest needs for acceptance, identity, security, and purpose?
2. Are you satisfied with your current approach to meeting your deepest needs? Why or why not?
3. How do you respond when your expectations are not met in a relationship? Are you more likely to feel frustration or anger, or do you react differently?
4. Think about the difference in results between trusting in people or things versus trusting in God. How has your marriage been affected by where you've placed your trust?
5. What would it look like to put your trust fully in Jesus and allow Him to meet your needs?

CONNECT WITH GOD

Father God, You created us to have a relationship with You and to have our deepest needs met in Jesus. You alone have the living water that satisfies our thirsty souls. Please forgive us for looking to other people or things to find acceptance, identity, security, and purpose. As we rely on Your faithful love, we believe that You will transform our hearts and marriages for our good and Your glory. In Jesus' name, Amen.

2

The Four Foundational Laws of Marriage

THE BIG IDEA
God's plan for marriage is absolutely perfect, and when your marriage is built on the foundation of His Word, you will be able to weather even the toughest storms.

REVIEW
In today's world, marriages often resemble turbulent and stormy seas. Couples long for a successful and fulfilling relationship, but few believe they can actually have one. True marital happiness seems impossible, so many people look to alternatives, such as staying single or cohabitating. And for those married couples who end up divorced, the results are devastating—emotional agony, social stigma, financial loss, and, of course, trauma for any children involved.

The disastrous conditions of marriage today are not necessary. Every bad marriage and subsequent divorce could be eliminated and replaced by a solid, satisfying relationship, if only each couple would follow God's plan.

God is the Creator, Inventor, and Designer of marriage, and He gives us the "instruction manual" in His Word. Genesis, the first book of the Bible, details how God created everything. He formed Adam from the dust of ground, and then from the place closest to Adam's heart (the rib), God made His most beautiful work: woman. From the very beginning God had a beautiful and perfect plan for marriage. That plan has never changed because God never changes.

Jesus said those who build their lives on His Word are like a wise man building on rock. When storms come, that house stands. But those who reject God's Word are like a foolish man building on sand. When storms come, that house crashes. It is no coincidence that today's society, which has rejected the Word of God, has such difficulty with marriage. If we reject God's Word, we cannot make marriage work, because it only works when we do it His way. Storms will still come, but marriages founded on God's truth will stand strong.

Genesis 2:24–25 is a short text with monumental implications. These verses serve as the initial record of God's design for marriage, and they contain four foundational laws crucial to marital success. Each law is essential to the success of the marriage relationship. Breaking even one of these laws can do serious damage to the marriage, and breaking multiple laws virtually guarantees disaster.

Let us carefully examine these verses:

> That is why a man leaves his father and mother and is united to his wife, and they become one flesh. Adam and his wife were both naked, and they felt no shame (Genesis 2:24–25).

This short passage may not appear to be "power packed," but it contains eternal and essential truths about marriage. God's few, well-chosen words have the power to transform ruined relationships. As you read the next four chapters with an open heart, I believe God will do something powerful in your life.

Scripture Reading

> Jesus Christ is the same yesterday and today and forever (Hebrews 13:8).

> "Therefore everyone who hears these words of mine and puts them into practice is like a wise man who built his house on the rock. The rain came down, the streams rose, and the winds blew and beat against that house; yet it did not fall, because it had its foundation on the rock.

But everyone who hears these words of mine and does not put them into practice is like a foolish man who built his house on sand. The rain came down, the streams rose, and the winds blew and beat against that house, and it fell with a great crash" (Matthew 7:24–27).

That is why a man leaves his father and mother and is united to his wife, and they become one flesh. Adam and his wife were both naked, and they felt no shame (Genesis 2:24–25).

> He sent out his word and healed them,
>   he rescued them from the grave
>   (Psalm 107:20).

Discussion Questions

1. In what ways has society been negatively affected by failing marriages? What impact has it had on our communities?
2. How can bad marriages and painful divorces be avoided?
3. How can Genesis 2:24–25 have so much importance and power when it's only two verses? How does this demonstrate God's nature?
4. Why is important to build our marriages on the foundation of God's Word rather than the world's system?

5. How have you seen the power of God's Word transform relationships?

Reflection Questions

1. What fears, doubts, or past hurts have influenced your view of relationships?
2. What passages of Scripture shape your beliefs about marriage? How do you apply these beliefs?
3. How does Genesis 2:24–25 provides a perfect design for marriage?
4. How can you and your spouse build your marriage on the solid foundation of God's Word?
5. Do you truly believe Jesus Christ is unchanging forever? How does this encourage you today? Thank Him for His eternal love.

Connect with God

Dear Father, I want Your Word to be the foundation of my life. I don't want to build my life on sand like the world does. Please give me a deeper love for Your Word as well as the wisdom to understand it and apply it to my life. Thank You for always being with me. I believe that Your plan for my life and my marriage is perfect. In Jesus' name, Amen.

3

The Law of Priority

THE BIG IDEA

God designed marriage to be the most important human relationship we have, second only to our personal relationship with him Most marital problems are caused by misplaced priorities.

REVIEW

God designed marriage as a covenant—a special commitment between a man and a woman that is more important than any other human relationship. In Genesis 2:24, God commands that a man should "leave" his father and mother when he becomes a husband. The Hebrew word for "leave" in this text is *azab*, which means to 'loosen or relinquish.' This "leaving" is not about abandoning or abusing one's parents; rather it means a man is to relinquish the highest position of commitment and devotion previously given to his parents in order to give that position to his wife. The wife become first, and the same instructions apply to the wife and her relationship with her parents. Of course, the husband and wife should continue to honor and respect both sets of parents.

God designed marriage to operate as the second most important priority in life, coming next to your personal relationship with Him. If we put marriage in any position of priority other than the one God has instituted, it does not work.

Problems in marriage are often the result of misplaced priorities, which can lead to frustrated and strife-filled lives and even divorce. Legitimate jealousy is the righteous emotion that causes us to protect what s rightfully ours. God put something inside us that makes us know our spouses belong to us before anyone or anything else, except Him. So when something threatens that correctly prioritized and pure element of our marriage, we feel legitimate jealousy.

There are forms of jealousy that are sinful and destructive, but in marriage, both spouses have moral obligations to God and to each other to protect their relationship from being violated by people or things of lesser priorities. When time, energy, or resources that rightfully belong to us are given by our spouse to someone or something else in any consistent or significant way, we will feel violated and experience legitimate jealousy. God Himself is the best example of this, as we see in Exodus 34:14 that one of His name is "Jealous." Because God loves us and created us to love Him before anyone or anything else, He becomes jealous when that relationship is threatened.

Couples highly prioritize their relationship leading up to the wedding. They believe that any issues will resolve once they are married. They invest time and attention in each other during the wedding and honeymoon phase, but as time passes, satisfaction usually begins to drop significantly. Why is this?

For a husband, the temptation may be to prioritize his career or hobbies over his marriage. For a wife, the temptation may be to give her all attention to the children or her own career. Regardless of the specifics, though, a person cannot allow anyone or anything to replace the priority of their spouse. If you do, you are violating God's design for marriage, and your partner is going to experience legitimate jealousy. If you do not correct the problem, it can seriously damage or even destroy your relationship.

Because so many people experience a downward trend of satisfaction in their marriages, they think it's an inevitable fact of life. But it is not! In fact, God designed marriage to get better every year. Although most people become less happy in their marriages year after year, it is certainly not because God made a mistake when He instituted marriage. It is because we made a mistake by failing to follow His plan.

If we will obey God's command to prioritize and keep our marriages higher than anything except our relationship with Him, then we can avoid a lot of unnecessary hurt and misery. Three steps can help establish and maintain correct priorities:

1. **List your priorities in order of importance.**
   Most lists of priorities should begin with God, move to your spouse, then your children (if applicable), your church, and so on.
2. **Prove your priorities through actions.**
   Both spouses must be willing to give up things to meet each other's needs. If you do not act upon your convictions, words will be of little use.
3. **Commit to protecting these priorities for the rest of your life.**
   Budget your time and energy. God gets the first and best, followed by your spouse, your children, and so on.

If you or your spouse has been expressing feelings of violation due to external influences in your marriage, heed these warning signals. These emotions arise to prevent the destruction of a sacred union designed by God for joy and blessings. By addressing the issues causing these feelings, you can reestablish

God's priorities in your marriage, leading to fulfillment and happiness.

SCRIPTURE READING

> That is why a man leaves his father and mother and is united to his wife, and they become one flesh. Adam and his wife were both naked, and they felt no shame (Genesis 2:24–25).
>
> Do not worship any other god, for the LORD, whose name is Jealous, is a jealous God (Exodus 34:14).
>
> "If you love me, keep my commands" (John 14:15).
>
> "But seek first the kingdom of God and His righteousness, and all these things shall be added to you" (Matthew 6:33 NKJV).

DISCUSSION QUESTIONS

1. What does the concept of "leaving" in Genesis 2:24 signify in God's design for marriage? Why is it important for the success of a marital relationship?
2. How can legitimate jealousy play a positive role in a marriage?
3. What are some common challenges that couples face after the initial excitement of the wedding and honeymoon, and how can they address these issues?

4. What are some practical ways for couples to protect their relationship from being violated by lesser priorities?
5. How can couples effectively allocate their time and energy to ensure they are prioritizing their relationship?

REFLECTION QUESTIONS

1. How do you honor your parents while keeping your spouse first?
2. In your own marriage, have you experienced a shift in priorities over time? How has this impacted the dynamics of your relationship?
3. Take some time to create a priority list. How will these priorities affect your decision-making and actions in your relationship?
4. How do your actions speak louder than words as you express love to your spouse?
5. Have you or your spouse felt violated by other things or other people invading your marriage? How will you respond to this warning signal?

CONNECT WITH GOD

Dear Father, thank You for the wonderful gift of my spouse. I repent for the times I have allowed other things and relationships to take a higher importance than my marriage. Today I commit to prioritizing my spouse above everything else except You. Give me wisdom, courage, and strengthen to live out this commitment through both my words and my actions for the rest of my life. In Jesus' name, Amen.

4

The Law of Pursuit

THE BIG IDEA

For the rest of your life, you must work every day at your marriage for it to be rewarding and healthy. When you stop working at it, it will stop working for you.

REVIEW

To understand how you can stay deeply and romantically in love for all of your married life or, for some, how to restore the love you have lost for your spouse, we must turn once again to Genesis 2:24–25. These verses emphasize the importance of understanding God's wisdom in setting the rules of marriage. After instructing us to "leave" (relinquish) our parents, God commands the husband to "cleave unto his wife" (Genesis 2:24 KJV).

The significance of this command lies in the literal meaning of "cleave" in Hebrew: 'to pursue with great energy and to cling to something zealously."[1]

God's directive to every husband is to zealously pursue and energetically cling to his wife for the rest of his life. The same principle holds true for the wife. Both spouse in a marriage should pursue and cling to each other.

From the very beginning, God revealed the secret to staying in love: **work**! Marriage only works when you work at it. The lack of effort in marriage is often the root cause of its decline. When spouses take one another for granted and try to rely solely on past memories and events, the relationship begins to slide backward.

Many people think that if they marry the right person, they should not have to work at the relationship to stay in love. This fallen world bombards us with deceptive notions of love and marriage. But if you think back to when you first fell in love, you will likely remember all the effort you put into the relationship. You wanted to impress our date, and you put in time and energy to try to please them. Chemistry can certainly be involved, but so is hard work. Only once the relationship seems secure do people start reducing their efforts and taking it for granted.

Living the same house, having the same kids, or sharing checkbook does not mean you will feel anything for your spouse or have a strong relationship. For the rest of your life, you must work every day at your marriage for it to be rewarding and healthy. When you stop working at it, it will stop working for you. Marriage is like muscles—the more we use them, the stronger the become, while the less we use them, the weaker they become.

It does not matter how "out of love" you are today. If you will begin to work at your relationship, you will soon see the resurrection of feelings and experiences that you thought were gone for good. Even if you have bad feelings toward your spouse, your feelings will change as you obey God's commandment to cleave. Don't put off until tomorrow what you need to do today.

You may think that a new relationship would be better. Some people have affairs that are going "so well" that they assume it's God's will. But affairs are always wrong in God's sight. Sin never solves any problems—it simply breeds newer and bigger ones.

If you will work hard at loving your spouse and meeting their needs (even if that spouse is not doing the same for you), you will begin to see a real difference in your marriage. And if both spouses commit to working hard at the marriage every day, the results will be incredible.

Perhaps you are in the stage where you have lost your love for each other and don't know how to heal your relationship. God has a guaranteed three-step plan to restore the first-love passion of your relationship, and we find it in Jesus' message to the church in Ephesus in Revelation 2:5: "Therefore, remember from where you have fallen, and repent, and do the deeds you did at first" (NASB).

1. "Therefore, remember from where you have fallen"
In the New Testament, the Greek word often used for "love" is *agape*. This word signifies "a commitment to love and do what is right for someone regardless of circumstances or emotions."[2] God's standard for love is rooted in unwavering commitment rather than fleeting feelings. Jesus doesn't say to stir up emotion. He knows love is a decision, not just a feeling. Reflect on the joyful details of your early relationship when both partners honored each other and were sensitive with their words. Recall the effort you put into impressing each other as well as the anticipation and preparation for time you spent together.

2. "Repent"
Repentance involves changing direction when we realize we are going the wrong way. If you sense the initial love you had in your marriage is fading, recognize that it's an indication something needs to change. Repentance requires acknowledging the truth, admitting wrongs, and taking corrective action.

3. "Do the deeds you did at first"
Jesus doesn't demand emotions, but He does tell us to act as we did at the beginning of the relationship. Invest time and energy into your relationship, regardless of your current feelings. Positive emotions and the "first love" will naturally return in time when the work is done.

Commit today to pursue your spouse with energy and diligence, rejecting the world's false concepts about love. You can have a marriage where love and satisfaction are the rule and not the exception if you are willing to obey God's commandment to cleave to your spouse.

SCRIPTURE READING

"And a man shall cleave unto his wife" (Genesis 2:24 KJV).

"Therefore, remember from where you have fallen, and repent, and do the deeds you did at first" (Revelation 2:4 NASB).

> Do not those who plot evil go astray?
> > But those who plan what is good find love and faithfulness.
> All hard work brings a profit,
> > but mere talk leads only to poverty
> > (Proverbs 14:22–23).

DISCUSSION QUESTIONS

1. How does the biblical command to "cleave" to your spouse challenge common misconceptions about love and marriage in today's society?
2. What are some reasons spouses eventually stop "cleaving" to each other?
3. Why do affairs fail to ultimately satisfy? How can couples safeguard their marriage against external temptations and maintain their commitment to each other?
4. How does working hard at the start of a relationship compare to later on? What typically changes?
5. What are some practical ways couples can apply the three steps to renewal (Remember, Repent, Do the Deeds You Did at First)?

REFLECTION QUESTIONS

1. Have you noticed a decline in passion or love over time in your marriage? What factors do you think contributed to this decline?
2. Consider your early experiences in dating your spouse. How did you invest time and energy into impressing each other? What specific memories that stand out?
3. What would "work" look like for you in your marriage today?

4. Which step to renewal do you find most challenging? How can you implement all three steps in your own life?
5. How do you think a renewed commitment to your marriage will affect your emotions?

CONNECT WITH GOD

Dear Father, we recognize that marriage is a blessing and a commitment. Please forgive us for the times we have taken our spouses for granted. Teach us to love them as You love us and help to pursue them as faithfully as You pursue us. We repent of any unforgiveness or bitterness. We invite you to work in our hearts and transform us into the husbands and wives You designed us to be. In Jesus' name, Amen.

5

The Law of Possession

THE BIG IDEA
Everything must be mutually surrendered and shared in marriage for true oneness. Selectively sharing some parts of yourself while withholding other areas causes mistrust, jealousy, and division.

REVIEW
Beyond the obvious meaning of becoming "one flesh" through sexual intercourse, Genesis 2:24 states a law of marriage that permeates every area of life. This law of possession is the key to establishing trust and intimacy in a relationship. Once we understand and obey this law, we will experience a significant depth of unity and bonding in marriage. However, if we break this law, even innocently, the damage to the trust and intimacy of the relationship can be severe, if not fatal.

Marriage is a complete union—all things previously owned and managed individually are now owned and managed jointly. There are no exceptions. Anything in marriage that is not willfully submitted to the ownership of the other person is held outside the union, producing legitimate jealousy. Becoming "one flesh" involves more than just physical intimacy. It involves merging everything owned by and associated with two persons into one mass, jointly owned and managed. If a spouse is unwilling to fully integrate something into the marriage, they are breaking the law of possession and violating the rights of their partner.

The apostle Paul provides insight into the law of possession in 1 Corinthians 7:3–4. This passage sheds light on the ownership of our bodies in marriage. It emphasizes the shift from personal ownership to shared ownership and control within the marital bond. This does not justify any form of abuse but underscores the reality that marriage requires the complete transfer of possession.

Anything that is not mutually owned and controlled by both partners will lead to division and problems. Each area of our marriage that we willingly surrender to joint ownership and control will build a spirit of trust and intimacy in the relationship.

The law of possession leaves no room for exceptions—it must encompass every facet of a successful marriage. Anything left outside of joint ownership and control threatens the sanctity of the marital bond. The violation of this law devastates many marriages and can be regarding any number of things. For some, the issue is money. For others, it is family. Still others struggle with careers, sports, education, time, future plans, children, and many other issues.

Jesus told His disciples that they must give up everything to follow Him (Luke 14:33). This means we must submit everything to His authority in order to follow Him. The same principle applies in marriage. When we withhold something from our spouse, it sends the message that the object or person in question is more important to us than they are. It implies a lack of trust in in our spouse.

Prenuptial agreements can be very problematic because they signify that not everything will be shared with one's future spouse. This blatantly violates the law of possession. Another common issue arises when a spouse accepts ownership of assets but not liabilities. In other words, they want the good but not the bad. Unless it is a sin or something illegal, you must accept ownership of everything in your spouse's life. Selective possession leads to hurt, mistrust and a loss of intimacy.

The greatest benefit of putting everything we have into marriage is that we now share everything. We belong to each other totally. Intimacy flows from a selfless, giving, sacrificial heart that is completely open and devoted to the object of its affection. Most members of today's society are desperately searching for intimacy in a relationship, but they are too selfish to pay the price.

The words "mine" and "yours" may work when you are single, but in marriage, a new vocabulary is required. These two little words can create issues, while "us" and "ours" can mend them. Marriage represents the complete sharing of life between two individuals—a lifelong commitment second only to one's eternal bond with the Creator. The price may seem steep, but it pales in comparison to the loneliness and disillusionment that accompany selfishness and personal protection. Dedicate everything to God and your spouse, and you'll discover that God's magnificent plan for marriage is beyond improvement.

SCRIPTURE READING

> That is why a man leaves his father and mother and is united to his wife, and they become one flesh. Adam and his wife were both naked, and they felt no shame (Genesis 2:24–25).

> The husband should fulfill his marital duty to his wife, and likewise the wife to her husband. The wife does not have authority over her own body but yields it to her husband. In the same way, the husband does not have authority over his own

body but yields it to his wife. Do not deprive each other except perhaps by mutual consent and for a time, so that you may devote yourselves to prayer (1 Corinthians 7:3–5).

"In the same way, those of you who do not give up everything you have cannot be my disciples" (Luke 14:33).

DISCUSSION QUESTIONS

1. How does the law of possession differ from our culture's push toward independence?
2. What are some things people often hold back or refuse to surrender in marriage? Why would withholding areas of your life from your spouse cause problems and mistrust?
3. How does the price of intimacy compare to the cost of maintaining independence?
4. How does the idea of shared ownership and control of one's body impact the dynamics of a marital relationship? Are there any potential challenges or misconceptions associated with this concept?
5. How can couples strike a balance between maintaining their individuality and fully committing to a shared life within a marriage?

REFLECTION QUESTIONS

1. How did you previously interpret the concept of "becoming one flesh" beyond sexual intercourse?
2. What areas have you been reluctant to share to your marriage?
3. Do you trust your spouse enough to share everything with them? If not, how can you build that trust together?
4. Do you use anything (sex, money, attention, etc.) to control your spouse? If so, are you willing to confess it as sin and repent to God and your spouse?
5. Take a moment to reflect on your own vocabulary and communication patterns within your relationship. Do you find yourself using possessive language, or do you consciously use inclusive terms? How might a shift in your language impact the dynamics of your marriage?

CONNECT WITH GOD

Dear Father, You have brought us together as one flesh. Please help us embrace the law of possession in our marriages, sharing not only our bodies but all aspects of our lives with our spouses. Give us grace as we build trust, intimacy, and a deep sense of partnership. We trust You, Lord, and we pray that our relationship will be a witness to Your goodness. In Jesus' name, Amen.

6

The Law of Purity

THE BIG IDEA
Purity is the atmosphere where love and intimacy find their deepest and most beautiful expression.

REVIEW
When God created Adam and Even in the Garden of Eden, He did not clothe them. He intended the first married couple to experience complete "nakedness" on all levels—physically, mentally, emotionally, and spiritually. In Genesis 2:25, we find them in a state of perfect openness and vulnerability before each other and before God. This state of complete exposure formed the foundation of what God envisions as a perfect marriage relationship.

In God's divine plan, marriage is the one relationship that allows true nakedness in every aspect of our lives: body, soul, and spirit. When we can reveal ourselves entirely to our spouses without shame or fear, we create a fertile ground for intimacy and connection to thrive. However, if we hide parts of ourselves, then there is a problem that needs to be addressed. God created us with a need for intimacy, and this can only be fulfilled in an atmosphere of honesty and vulnerability.

Healthy nakedness must happen in a special place with the right person. Although special friends and family can accommodate the need for exposure to some degree, marriage is the singular place God has created for us to fulfill the need for total exposure of our true selves.

Even if your current situation makes it challenging to embrace this level of openness and vulnerability, yet the truth remains: God created a need in mankind for complete exposure, and He made marriage as the place for this need to be met.

Before Adam and Eve sinned, they were able to expose themselves completely to God and to each other. But when they ate the forbidden fruit, their innocence instantly gave way to shame and fear, and they gathered fig leaves to cover their genitals. No longer could their differences be openly expressed or their most sensitive areas exposed without fear. They no longer had unhindered intimacy.

In any relationship, sin is the single greatest hindrance to the ability to openly relate to one another. This is where the law of purity applies. The description of Adam and Eve's being naked and unashamed was not written to show us the original purity of mankind and of marriage. Sin disrupts our ability to connect openly with one another, and we must understand these three facts:

1. **Sin is always deadly.**
   Sin deviates from God's design, and while it may provide temporary pleasure, it initiates a destructive process. The key is to stop sin at its inception, just as Adam and Eve's disobedience started with the devil's deception.

2. **Purity must be upheld by both partners.**
   For a marriage to have an atmosphere of complete exposure, both spouses must commit to purity. This means maintaining purity in thoughts, actions, and intentions.

3. **Purity encompasses every area.**
   Purity applies to every facet of life—not just physical actions but also thoughts, emotions, and intentions.

To establish and maintain purity in marriage, here are seven steps to consider:

1. **Take responsibility for your own behavior.**
   You cannot change your spouse's actions, but you can work on yourself with God's guidance. Build an atmosphere of purity and trust from your side first.

2. **Do not return sin for sin.**
   Revenge and retaliation only perpetuate problems in a marriage. Respond with love and goodness. When you fight fire with fire you just get a bigger fire!
3. **Admit your faults.**
   Admitting when you are wrong and asking for forgiveness can have a profound impact on healing a marriage. The cycle of purity begins in marriage when one spouse admits that he or she has been wrong.
4. **Forgive.**
   Forgiveness is vital in marriage, as it not only aligns with God's command but also prevents bitterness from poisoning your heart.
5. **Speak the truth in love.**
   Address concerns openly and lovingly with your spouse. Avoiding issues or letting them fester is detrimental your relationship.
6. **Pray for each other.**
   Only God can effect change in your spouse's life. Pray for them sincerely and with love rather than trying to manipulate, intimidate, or dominate.
7. **Seek righteous friends and fellowship.**
   Surround yourself with friends and influences who align with your commitment to purity in

marriage. The company you keep can significantly impact your relationship.

Seek to make your home and marriage a safe space where both you and your spouse can "get naked." Seek God's will daily, as well as His forgiveness and guidance. Practicing honesty, accountability, and forgiveness toward one another. By respecting God's law of purity in marriage, you will witness a transformation in the atmosphere and pleasure of your relationship. Purity becomes the fertile ground where love and intimacy find their deepest and most beautiful expression.

SCRIPTURE READING:

> That is why a man leaves his father and mother and is united to his wife, and they become one flesh. Adam and his wife were both naked, and they felt no shame (Genesis 2:24–25).

> "Blessed are the pure in heart,
>   for they will see God" (Matthew 5:8).

> You were taught, with regard to your former way of life, to put off your old self, which is being corrupted by its deceitful desires; to be made new in the attitude of your minds; and to put on the new self, created to be like God in true righteousness and holiness. Therefore each of you must

put off falsehood and speak truthfully to your neighbor, for we are all members of one body (Ephesians 4:22–25).

DISCUSSION QUESTIONS

1. How does the biblical concept of Adam and Eve's "complete nakedness" in the Garden of Eden relate to the idea of openness and vulnerability in modern marriages?
2. Why is it important to understand that marriage is the relationship that allows for the highest degree of "nakedness" on all levels—physically, mentally, emotionally, and spiritually?
3. Why is sin the greatest obstacle to openness and purity in marriage? How can recognizing and addressing sin help couples build a healthy relationship?
4. What are some potential consequences when spouses refuse to forgive each other?
5. How can the wrong kinds of friends and influences negatively impact a marriage?

REFLECTION QUESTIONS

1. How "naked' are you in your marriage today? How "naked" would you like to be?

2. In what ways do sin or unhealthy behaviors obstruct intimacy in your relationship with your spouse?
3. How do you respond when your spouse shares their vulnerabilities or mistakes with you?
4. How can you better communicate your feelings and thoughts to your spouse in a loving and honest manner?
5. How do the relationships and influences around you impact the purity and health of your marriage?

CONNECT WITH GOD

Dear Father, nothing is hidden from Your sight. You call us to walk in complete openness and vulnerability in our marriages. Forgive us for when we have violated the law of purity by tolerating sin in our lives. Cleanses us and help us to move forward together in honesty, forgiveness, and love. Thank You that we do not have to live in fear or shame one moment longer. In Jesus' name, Amen.

7

God's Blueprint for Marital Bliss

THE BIG IDEA

God's design for marriage is sacrificial, servant-hearted men and honoring, caring women. A blissful, biblical marriage beings by putting faith in God's Word and believing it has the answers you seek.

REVIEW

What is your idea of a perfect mate? Excluding some minor personal preferences, both sexes have universal standards for what they desires from the opposite sex. For many men, the ideal woman is someone who makes him feel like a king. This "cheerleader" not only admires and supports him but also fulfills his sexual desires. She looks her best all the time and creates a welcoming home environment while also sharing his hobbies and interests.

For many women, the ideal man is sensitive and affectionate. He actively contributes to the well-being of their home and treats her as an equal when making decisions. He opens up to her and communicates with her intimately and honestly. He works hard and provides for her financially, and he is both generous and wise with money.

The apostle Paul writes about the ideal mate in Ephesians 5:21–33. This blueprint for marital bliss unveils the kind of marriage that God envisions for His people. When couples seek marriage counseling, it's not because they have a problem with the instructions for their spouse. Rather, they object to the instructions for themselves.

There are three general reasons why people resist making changes in their own lives:

1. **Fear of Going First**
   They are afraid to commit to their own biblical roles until their spouses change. They fear being taken advantage of if they become vulnerable. The more pride and hurt are present in the relationship, the more stubborn the standoff.

2. **Society's Influence**
   Society models a perverted image of masculinity, causing men to reject their God-given roles as sacrificial servants. Women respond bitterly to the notion of submission. It's important to

note that God created men and women as loving equals who supply what the other needs.

3. **Lack of Faith**
   In some instances, spouses just don't believe biblical roles will work in their marriage. If they believe in the Bible and understand that their current efforts aren't working, then the next logical step is to put their faith in God's Word.

If we can get past the hindrances that keep us from seeing the picture clearly, we will begin to understand that the way God designed marriage is perfect. In fact, the description of marriage in Ephesians chapter five is the description of a dream marriage, where both partners are doing exactly what the other person wants and needs him or her to do.

The proper roles of husbands and wives found in Ephesians 5:21–33 accomplish three things:

1. **Biblical Roles Provide**
   No one can meet their own needs completely; otherwise, marriage would be unnecessary. When spouses fulfill their biblical roles, they meet many of each other's needs. Men need honor, and women need security.

2. **Biblical Roles Protect**
   When husbands and wives fulfill their roles, both spouses have their needs met, and they feel protected. The longer one spouse refuses

to do it God's way, the more they encourage the other spouse to do the same.

3. **Biblical Roles Promote**
When both spouses love one another as described in Ephesians 5, the results are deeper love, intimacy, and trust. This keeps the relationship growing year after year. Neglecting these roles leads to deterioration and transforms a dream marriage into a nightmare.

How many unhealthy marriages do you know that involve two individuals who love each other as the Bible describes? The answer is probably none. On the contrary, most troubled marriages can be traced back to individuals who fail to fulfill their biblical roles.

The truth is, marriage still works, and it can be wonderful. God's design calls for sacrificial, servant men and honoring, caring women. Their selfless love for each other is meant to sustain their relationship throughout life.

A blissful, biblical marriage begins by putting faith in God's Word and believing that it has the answers you seek. Obedience by faith is the key to experiencing the love and fulfillment He designed us to enjoy.

As you give, your love will multiply. As you serve, God will honor and bless you. By laying down your life for your spouse, you'll discover the life you've been seeking. There's no need to delay any longer. Build your marriage according to God's blueprint, and your dream marriage awaits.

SCRIPTURE READING

> Submit to one another out of reverence for Christ. Wives, submit yourselves to your own husbands as you do to the Lord. For the husband is the head of the wife as Christ is the head of the church, his body, of which he is the Savior. Now as the church submits to Christ, so also wives should submit to their husbands in everything. Husbands, love your wives, just as Christ loved the church and gave himself up for her to make her holy, cleansing her by the washing with water through the word, and to present her to himself as a radiant church, without stain or wrinkle or any other blemish, but holy and blameless. In this same way, husbands ought to love their wives as their own bodies. He who loves his wife loves himself (Ephesians 5:21–28).

> "Do not judge, and you will not be judged. Do not condemn, and you will not be condemned. Forgive, and you will be forgiven. Give, and it will be given to you. A good measure, pressed down, shaken together and running over, will be poured into your lap. For with the measure you use, it will be measured to you" (Luke 6:37–38).

DISCUSSION QUESTIONS

1. How does society influence our view of gender roles? How does this compare with Paul's description in Ephesians chapter 5?
2. Why do you think people often resist fulfilling their own biblical roles even though they want their spouse to fulfill theirs?
3. What are examples of ways a husband can meet his wife's deepest need? How can a wife meet her husband's deepest need?
4. In what ways have you seen biblical roles promote intimacy and growth when applied?
5. How would society improve if husbands and wives followed biblical roles? How would divorce rates be affected?

REFLECTION QUESTIONS

1. How closely does your idea of a perfect spouse align with the descriptions in this chapter?
2. How do you currently fulfill the biblical roles described in Ephesians chapter 5 in your own marriage?
3. In what areas of your relationship with your spouse do you need to demonstrate more faith and trust in God's design?
4. What steps can you take to break the cycle of unmet needs and frustrations in your marriage?

5. How does your marriage reflect the mutual submission and respect described in the Bible?

CONNECT WITH GOD

Dear Father, we want our marriages to reflect Your perfect design that You give us in Your Word. We repent of any fear, stubbornness, or unbelief, and we choose today to embrace our biblical roles as husbands and wives. Help us, Lord, as we partner with You to meet our spouses' deepest needs. We believe that as we follow Your Word, our marriages will grow and thrive for the rest of our lives. In Jesus' name, Amen.

8 & 9

The Destructive Husband & Four Kinds of Destructive Husbands

THE BIG IDEA

When men righteously steward their responsibility and use their influence to protect and provide for those in their care, their spouses and children will reflect appreciation and contentment through their behavior.

REVIEW

The greatest single factor hurting relationships between the sexes is unrighteous men. Men must realize they have been entrusted by God to lead their families, churches, and society as a whole. Whenever men righteously steward this responsibility and use their influence to protect and provide for those in their care, their spouses and children will reflect appreciation and contentment through their behavior.

Our love for Jesus is not primarily driven by commandments or threats but by His selfless sacrifice on the cross. We are drawn to Him because He willingly gave His life for us. Similarly, women are drawn to men who exhibit sacrificial love and meet their needs, not out of obligation but out of genuine care and love. Nothing endears a man to a woman more than the quality of sacrificial love, just as nothing embitters a woman more than a selfish or abusive man.

This does not mean that women lack independent thoughts or are merely reacting to their husbands. Women are created by God as equal to men in every spiritual, moral, and intellectual sense. While women differ emotionally and physically from men, they are not inferior or superior. They possess unique intelligence and have been purposefully designed by God to fulfill a distinct role in life.

To better understand the impact of men on society and relationships, think about the stories in the Old Testament about the kings of Israel. When the kings acted righteously, the people flourished. However, when the kings were unrighteous and rebellious, the people suffered as they adopted the same sinful attitude.

Four Kinds of Destructive Husbands

The Dominant Husband

King Rehoboam, Solomon's son and successor, tried to dominate the people of Israel into submission because he refused to humble himself. The results were disastrous. A dominant husband exerts excessive control and authority over his family, stifling their individuality and autonomy. This leads to a sense of oppression and unhappiness. A true leader has a servant's heart, and the choices husbands make will determine not only their leadership style but also whom they lead. God wants men to be loving leaders, not petty tyrants.

Boys need physical affection, affirmation, and attention from their parents. Without this nurturing, they might develop an overly strong personality, leading to codependent relationships where they dominate partners with low self-esteem. Dominant parental influences can also lead to personality issues. These negative traits (iniquities) can perpetuate dysfunctional patterns in families and must be broken and cleaned through accepting responsibility for one's behavior, identifying the problem, repenting, forgiving the parents, and actively breaking negative patterns. Dominant men can be influenced by ignorance and insecurity as well as sin and deception. Finally, some men have a dominant temperament that if not submitted to God can lead to abusive behavior.

The Passive Husband

King Ahab was an ungodly king who allowed his evil wife, Jezebel, to terrorize God's people. A passive husband may seem sweet and sensitive at first, but his refusal to lead will destroy any sense of security and respect the wife once had for him.

Some passive men were dominated by their parents during childhood and never learned to act for themselves. Passive men tend to gravitate toward dominant women, but resentment eventually builds because neither spouse has their needs met. Men can also be intimidated by the fear of doing the wrong thing, so they refuse to take their place as loving, sacrificial leaders. Some passive men torment their wives with silence and inaction, while others are simply too lazy to take responsibility. Finally, a man may have a laid-back personality, but this becomes a problem when he fails to lead his family as directed by God's Word.

The Immoral Husband

King David was a great leader and warrior, but he made the terrible choice to commit adultery with Bathsheba, followed by the next terrible choice of having her husband murdered. Immorality is a growing problem because sin can never be satisfied—the more you get, the more you want. The more you indulge, the more it takes to satisfy. The devil always over-promises and under-delivers because his only desire is to destroy your life and marriage.

Some immoral behavior stems from a lack of physical and emotional affection in childhood. Men are very visual beings, and God designed them to be attracted to their wives. But the world tries to manipulate men's basic sexual instincts through explicit imagery. Long before sexual sin occurs, there are undisciplined eyes looking lustfully. When men see erotic images, the chemical epinephrine release in their brains and locks in those images. A man can never overcome lust until he wins the battle for his mind by meditating on God's Word. Every word in the Bible is nuclear in the realm of the Spirit, and if you fight the battle with God's Word, you will win!

Millions of men live in sexual deception because they think that pornography, adultery, and other forms of sexual sin will satisfy them. But it is a lie! The greatest sexual pleasure a man will ever experience is in a sexually pure, monogamous, loving relationship with his wife.

The Distracted Husband

King Solomon was the wisest man who ever lived, but when he stopped pursing a relationship with God, his distracted and driven existence left him spiritually and emotionally bankrupt. Many men equate acceptance with performance, and this often begins in childhood. Yes, it is important to be responsible, but anything that compromises one's relationship with God, wife, or family isn't of God.

Some men hide behind the excuse providing for their family when they're actually doing it for themselves. The only answer to greed is repentance, and the same is true for wrong values and priorities. Work is supposed to support the home, not the other way around. If a man spends his life building a relationship with God, his wife, children, and grandchildren he will be a happy and successful man.

Unresolved conflict at home can lead men to gravitate toward their workplace to have their basic needs met. But the only real answer is to repent and go home. God will always honor men who persevere in prayer and face their challenges head on.

SCRIPTURE READING

> Husbands, love your wives, just as Christ loved the church and gave himself up for her to make her holy, cleansing her by the washing with water

through the word, and to present her to himself as a radiant church, without stain or wrinkle or any other blemish but holy and blameless. In the same way, husbands ought to love their wives as their own bodies. He who loves his wife loves himself. After all, no one ever hated their own body, but they feed and care for their body, just as Christ does the church (Ephesians 5:25–29).

"Whoever wants to become great among you must be your servant, and whoever wants to be first must be your slave—just as the Son of Man did not come to be served, but to serve, and to give his life as a ransom for many" (Matthew 20:26–28).

"For I, the Lord your God, am a jealous God, visiting the iniquity of the fathers upon the children to the third and fourth generations of those who hate Me" (Deuteronomy 5:9 NKJV).

For the wages of sin is death, but the gift of God is eternal life in Christ Jesus our Lord (Romans 6:23).

> I made a covenant with my eyes
> not to look lustfully at a young woman
> (Job 31:1).

DISCUSSION QUESTIONS

1. How does the concept of sacrificial love, as mentioned in Ephesians 5:25, challenge the traditional views of masculinity in our society?

2. Reflecting on the idea that a spouse tends to mirror their partner's character and behavior, what are some ways individuals can ensure they are positively influencing their partners?
3. What are the differences between a dominant and passive husbands? What are the similarities?
4. In what ways have you seen the destructive kinds of husbands celebrated in contemporary society? How does this conflict with biblical teaching?
5. How can a couple maintain a healthy balance of leadership and partnership in their marriage?

PERSONAL REFLECTION QUESTIONS

1. How have unrighteous men impacted your own life or community? Are there any hurts you need to forgive?
2. What iniquities do you recognize in your family? Ask the Lord to help you release and break them today.
3. How do you and your spouse handle conflict? Is this a healthy or unhealthy method?
4. How would sacrificial love and leadership impact your relationship with your spouse?

5. What mentors or leaders in your life would be a good source of wisdom and guidance, especially during challenging times?

CONNECT WITH GOD

Dear Father, we come to You with humble hearts, seeking Your guidance and wisdom. We recognize that You created men to be loving and sacrificial servant-leaders and that true masculinity is a gift. We repent for the destructive behaviors we have allowed into our lives and marriages. Your way is the only path to true happiness and fulfillment, and we commit to following it every day of our lives. In Jesus' name, Amen.

10

How to Understand and Meet Your Wife's Needs

THE BIG IDEA

The four essential needs of every women are security, nonsexual affection, open communication, and leadership. When husbands recognize and work energetically to meet these needs, the result is a healthy, fulfilling relationship.

REVIEW

When a man marries a woman, he receives a precious gift from God, and this gift requires care and attention. In order to have a happy marriage, a husband must understand two things: his wife is different than him (even beyond the obvious physical and sexual differences), and she has four major needs that he is responsible to meet.

Both sexes need to realize that neither is weird or wrong. We are simply the way God created us. We can choose to accept these differences and learn to serve one another or we can continue generations of frustration and conflict. Marriage the way God designed it is a win-win proposition, and spouses become best friends and intimate lovers. But rejection and accusation in a marriage causes spouse to become bitter rivals and mutual victims.

The four basic needs of a woman are security, soft and nonsexual affection, open and honest communication, and leadership.

Security

Security is a woman's greatest need. She needs to feel safe and well-provided for in every aspect of her life. Even though a woman's deepest need for security is provided by God alone there is a dimension of her security that is met by God through her husband. To fulfill this role effectively, a husband must communicate four things to his wife:

1. He cares for her above anyone or anything except God.

When a woman senses her husband is preoccupied or detached in some way, she will immediately feel insecure. She can discern instinctively if her husband is truly caring for her. The best way a husband can determine if he is caring for his wife properly is simply to ask her! Committing yourself to meeting your wife's needs doesn't mean you lose your authority or manhood. True and lasting authority is built upon the foundation of sacrificial servanthood. It is leadership by example, not ego.

2. He admires and loves her.

A woman thrives in an atmosphere of praise and adoration. When you praise your wife and convince her of your love in real ways, you earn the right to also confront her in love. But if you only point out her flaws, she will become insecure and bitter toward you.

Here are some simple rules for praising your wife:

- Say something positive about your wife multiple times a day.
- Say something about every area of her life, not just her looks.
- Never use sarcasm or backhanded compliments.
- Earn your words of correction.
- Be romantic and demonstrate your love and respect.

3. He is faithful.

Adultery is not simply a physical act; it is an attitude. A man's heart must remain faithful, not just when his wife is present, but also when she is absent. Tell your wife on a regular basis that she is the only one you desire. Don't compare her to other women or watch other women. Never threaten to cheat on or leave your wife out of anger or frustration.

4. *He is dedicated to providing financially for her.*

Finances are one of the most important areas of security for a woman. A husband communicates this commitment by praying for God's blessing and direction, seeking the best employment possible, working hard, and wisely managing money.

Soft, Nonsexual Affection

All women need soft nonsexual affection. Affectionate gestures like hugging, holding hands, and cuddling a wife feel cherished, and children feel secure when they see affection between their parents. Specifically ask what your wife desires in the area of affection and then do what she requests.

Open and Honest Communication

Wives have a legitimate need for detailed and honest communication. Sharing information is one of the most powerful ways a wife is made to feel one with her husband. It is her way of connecting with him. Communication is as important to women as sex is to men. When a husband doesn't open up and tell his wife what he is doing, feeling, or thinking, she becomes insecure and frustrated, which opens the door to the enemy's deception. Open and honest communication is essential for marital success. There is no such thing as the strong, silent type—true strength is displayed in the courage to open up, not in hiding thoughts and feelings in fear.

Leadership

Regardless of how passive or dominant a woman is, she has a deep desire to be led by a caring, righteous man. This doesn't mean she wants to be dominated or controlled. Rather, she wants her husband to lead the family in faith, finances, discipline, romance, and every other area. When a man does not exercise such leadership, his wife becomes insecure and frustrated. Again, men and women are totally equal, and leadership by men doesn't mean they are better or have greater rights than their wives. Husbands lead because it is God's design, and this leadership meets a deep need as long as the wives are treated with equality and respect.

SCRIPTURE READING

> In this same way, husbands ought to love their wives as their own bodies. He who loves his wife loves himself. After all, no one ever hated their own body, but they feed and care for their body, just as Christ does the church (Ephesians 5:28–29).

"Anyone who looks at a woman lustfully has already committed adultery with her in his heart" (Matthew 5:28).

You, my brothers and sisters, were called to be free. But do not use your freedom to indulge the flesh; rather, serve one another humbly in love. For the entire law is fulfilled in keeping this one command: "Love your neighbor as yourself" (Galatians 5:13–14).

DISCUSSION QUESTIONS

1. How can husband and wives learn to accept and embrace their differences?
2. What are some practical ways husbands can actively demonstrate their care and commitment to their wives?
3. What role does open and honest communication play in a healthy marriage?
4. What are the dangers of comparing one's spouse to others?
5. How can men lead in a way that is respectful and empowering to their wives?

REFLECTION QUESTIONS

1. How do you handle differences in your marriage? Are you accepting and understanding, or are you condescending and rejecting?

2. How do you show your spouse that you are 100 percent committed to them?
3. Do you feel comfortable with soft, nonsexual affection, or do you and your spouse need to grow in this area?
4. How often do you praise and verbally honor your spouse?
5. In what ways can you improve the spiritual leadership in your home?

CONNECT WITH GOD

Dear Father, You designed men and women perfectly and differently. Help us to honor those differences in one another and to appreciate our spouses as Your incredible creation. Help us as husbands to love our wives as Christ loves the Church and to meet their needs to the best of our ability. Guide us to speak words of love and encouragement, to remain pure in our thoughts and actions, and to lead our families with wisdom and integrity. In Jesus' name, Amen.

11 & 12

The Destructive Wife & Four Kinds of Destructive Wives

THE BIG IDEA
It doesn't matter how bad your problems are or how long you have had them; the only thing that matters is God's great power and love for us. Only God can and will take a destructive man or woman and change him or her into a vessel of love and honor.

REVIEW
Just as men possess their share of destructive tendencies, women also have natural but unhealthy weaknesses that can damage relationships. The longer these base instincts are allowed in a marriage, the more they deteriorate the inner core of the relationship. The passion, intimacy, and goodwill of the

marriage fade away as toxic emotions such as anger, resentment, and hopelessness take their place.

In John chapter 4, the Samaritan woman at the well need Jesus' help to heal the inner issues that caused her multiple failed marriages. When we don't have a daily, dependent relationship with God, we automatically transfer the expectations of our deepest needs to our spouses and those closest to us. In so doing, we set up the relationship for disappointment and failure.

Four Kinds of Destructive Wives

1. The Dominant Wife

God designed marriage to have a healthy dependent/codependent relationship. The wife is meant to depend on her husband, while he, in turn, relies on her dependency. This arrangement allows her to feel feminine, protected, and cherished, while he experiences masculinity, importance, and need. Consequently, she feels loved, and he feels respected. But when the roles are reversed, the couple experiences a disorienting power struggle, and both partners will eventually push each other away.

A woman may become a dominant wife because her rebellious sin nature wants to control her husband. Or she may be afraid that if she does not take and keep control, there will be negative results.

A woman may have grown up with a detached or under-nurturing father who did not provide affection and affirmation, so she overcompensated to fill that void. There may have been wrong training as the women in her family dominated the men and passed this iniquity through the generations. Finally, some women have a naturally strong and aggressive personality. A wife's strong temperament can be a wonderful complement to her husband's authority when it is submitted to and led by God's Spirit. When it is not, her temperament can cause her to usurp her husband's authority, which deeply damages the essence of the marriage bond.

2. The Enabler

Any time one allows or provides for the destructive behavior of a person in one's family or of someone close, they are an enabler. The opposite of an enabler is a person who refuses to watch, allow, or help another person self-destruct. They also stand up to abuse toward themselves or others.

When enabling tendencies stem from low self-esteem, the solution is stop believing what everyone else has to say and start believing what the Word of God says. Words of criticism and discouragement must give way to words of comfort and praise. A distorted view of love must be corrected by breaking any inner vows and understanding that love includes care, correction, and confrontation. Some women become enablers because they fear rejection and isolation, but we must remember that God never rejects us for doing what is right. Even the most laid-back women must learn to stand up for herself and speak the truth in love.

3. The Distracted Wife

A wife may become distracted as she tries to fill the void left by her distracted husband. She may find herself giving higher priority to her children because the job of motherhood is more demanding or even more fulfilling. She may feel overloaded by stress and responsibilities, both in her family life and in her professional career. Relationships with friends, parents, and other family members can threaten the marriage when they take too much of the wife's attention away from her husband. In order to fight for the marriage, a woman must turn her heart toward her husband and faithfully protect the time and energy he deserves, even if it means sacrificing other relationships or activities.

4. The Emotion-Motivated Wife

In 2 Timothy 3:6, the apostle Paul speaks about "weak-willed women" who are led by their emotions and external influences instead of their convictions. These women are vulnerable because they rely on their feelings instead of the truth when making decisions. The answer to this dilemma is to do what is right regardless of what our feelings say. Feelings may be real, but that doesn't mean they are right. Make God's Word the engine to motivate your actions now, and you will find that proper feelings will follow later.

To break out of the bondage of being weak-willed and emotion-motivated, women need to know the major causes of this problem include unbelief, a lack of discipline, and deception (or wrong information). They must repent and obey what God says, allowing His Word to determine their life's parameters and rejecting Satan's lies. When we read God's Word, it fills our minds with truth that solves our problems and makes our lives pleasant and productive.

SCRIPTURE READING

> A wife of noble character who can find?
>   She is worth far more than rubies.
> Her husband has full confidence in her
>   and lacks nothing of value.
> She brings him good, not harm,
>   all the days of her life (Proverbs 31:10–12).

> Better to live on a corner of the roof
>   than share a house with a quarrelsome wife
>   (Proverbs 21:9).

Teach the older women to be reverent in the way they live, not to be slanderers or addicted to much wine, but to teach what is good. Then they can urge the younger women to love their husbands and children, o be self-controlled and pure, to be busy at home, to be kind, and to be subject to their husbands, so that no one will malign the word of God (Titus 2:3–5).

> A wife of noble character is her husband's crown, but a disgraceful wife is like decay in his bones (Proverbs 12:4).

DISCUSSION QUESTIONS

1. How can couples work together to ensure they are not placing unrealistic expectations on each other?
2. How can a spouse prone to enabling break free from the cycle without becoming dominant?
3. What are some common distractions that lead to conflict in a marriage?
4. In what ways can a distorted view of love affect a marriage?
5. How can spouses strike a balance between acknowledging their emotions and making rational decisions in relationships?

REFLECTION QUESTIONS

1. In what ways have your upbringing and past experiences shaped your approach to marriage?
2. How do you handle criticism or feedback in your relationship with your spouse?
3. Consider the balance between your roles as a spouse, parent, and individual. Are there areas where you need to reassess your priorities?
4. How does your faith influence your relationships? Are there areas where you need to strengthen your faith to improve your relationships?
5. Have you ever felt that you or your spouse were distracted from your marriage? What were the underlying causes, and how did it affect your relationship?

CONNECT WITH GOD

Dear Father, You are the God of hope and healing. We admit that we are imperfect people who need Your help to succeed in our relationships with each other. Cover our marriages with Your grace as we put away unhealthy patterns and walk forward in faith. We reject every lie of the enemy. May Your Word be the light to our path, and may our homes be filled Your peace and joy. In Jesus' name, Amen.

13

How to Understand and Meet Your Husband's Needs

THE BIG IDEA
A man's four greatest needs are honor, sex, friendship with his wife, and domestic support. By adopting a respectful, loving, and supportive approach, wives provide an environment for their husbands to thrive.

REVIEW
Queen Esther was a beautiful, strong woman with a teachable, humble spirit, and God used her to protect His chosen people from annihilation. To be successful in marriage, wives must realize that honor is crucial. In our society, it's popular to dishonor, but this approach only damages marriages. Husbands *need* honor more than anything else. Regardless of the status of your relationship today, God's Word is powerful enough to do miracles.

The four basic needs of a man are honor, sex, friendship with his wife, and domestic support.

1. Honor

Honor is a man's greatest need. In his letter to the Ephesians, Paul told wives to "submit yourselves to your own husbands as you do to the Lord" (Ephesians 5:22). The standard of a wife's behavior in marriage is to treat her husband as she would treat Jesus, even though no man can truly match up to the divine standard.

There is an important difference between suffering and abuse. Suffering means discomfort, but abuse means damage. Abuse includes anything that causes real damage to a woman and/or her children (whether mental, emotional, sexual, or physical). One of the greatest sins a man can commit against God is to abuse a woman or child. An abusive man needs to be confronted and challenged about his behavior, and appropriate steps must be taken to protect the woman and the children.

Here are some ways to demonstrate honor:

- **Allow him to fail.**

    A true test of honor is how a wife responds when her husband fails, which he will do sometimes. Progress is only made through honor and support. Wives can express disagreements in an honoring way, but then they must trust the Holy Spirit to be the enforcer.

- **Honor him at the level where you want him to be.**
- Proverbs 31 describes the virtuous woman as a model wife and mother. Her husband's status as an elder in the community is attributed to her behavior toward him. This suggests that her treatment of him contributed to his honor and accomplishments. Your husband will rise to the level of your praise and honor. The best way to get your husband's attention is by honor. The best way to change your husband is by honor. The best way to get your husband to desire you and spend time with you is by honor.

- **Cover his faults and reflect his strengths.**
While a wife must be able to communicate her concerns privately, she should refrain from exposing his weaknesses in front of others.. Let him know that he can trust you to honor him and cover his faults.

2. Sex

Sex is a powerful force in a man's life, and as a wife, you are the only legitimate source for satisfying your husband's needs. Rejecting these needs can make him feel rejected as a person and leave him vulnerable to temptation. To understand how a wife can aggressively meet her husband's need for sex, consider these suggestions:

- **Understand the strength and importance of the male appetite for sex.**
  Understand and accept your husband's need for sex. Instead of making him plead or feel guilty, approach him with a commitment to meet his needs. This creates a powerful bond of love and trust. (Likewise, a husband should be just as committed to meeting his wife's sexual needs.) Any refusal must be done in a sensitive, godly way.

- **Understand the visual and physical nature of a man's sexual appetite.**
  Men get sexually excited much faster than women, mostly through sight and touch. This is why men are drawn to erotic images. Wives should avoid comparisons, which is self-rejecting. While it is healthy to want to look your best, it's best to accept who you. Modesty is valuable, but don't let it interfere in the bedroom. Even if you don't understand what about your body turns him on, rest assured that it really does.

- **Be creative and sensitive.**
  Wives should make regular efforts to be creative and aggressive in the bedroom. Plan and

create opportunities for such moments. Be sensitive to your husband and don't make him beg for sex.

3. Friendship with His Wife

A strong desire to spend time together is a positive sign for your marriage. If you have different interests, there are ways to compromise:

- **Make an effort to be involved with your husband in the things he enjoys.**
  Do your best to be interested and involved as much as you can in the things he enjoys. This is a powerful way to deepen your friendship, fun, and intimacy together. Without sex and fun, marriage is a business relationship.

- **Do not mother your husband.**
  It's easy to treat your husband like one of the kids when he's acting like them, but your husband does not need for you to be his mother. He needs for you to be his lover, friend, and helpmate.

4. Domestic Support

A man's home is the place he goes to find honor and fulfillment. When his home no longer provides these, he may look elsewhere for satisfaction. Domestic support doesn't mean women should bear all household responsibilities; men should contribute equally. However, women excel at creating a warm, inviting home atmosphere. Whether you work outside the home or not, maintaining a domestic focus and nurturing the home environment is crucial for your husband.

SCRIPTURE READING

> Wives, submit yourselves to your own husbands as you do to the Lord. For the husband is the head of the wife as Christ is the head of the church, his body, of which he is the Savior. Now as the church submits to Christ, so also wives should submit to their husbands in everything (Ephesians 5:22–24).

> May your fountain be blessed,
>   and may you rejoice in the wife of your youth.
> A lovely doe, a graceful deer—
>   may her breasts satisfy you always,
>   may you ever be intoxicated with her love
> (Proverbs 5:18–19).

> He who finds a wife finds what is good
>   and receives favor from the LORD
> (Proverbs 18:22).

DISCUSSION QUESTIONS

1. What are some practical ways a wife can demonstrate honor for her husband?

2. How can the concept of allowing a husband to fail be helpful in a marriage?
3. What role does friendship play in a marriage, and how can it be nurtured?
4. How can wives avoid the pitfall of mothering their husbands?
5. How can couples work together to ensure that the home remains a place of honor and fulfillment for both partners, and what role should each spouse play in achieving this goal?

REFLECTION QUESTIONS

1. How do you typically respond when your husband faces challenges or makes mistakes? Is there room for improvement?
2. Have there been times when you or your husband felt that his sexual needs were not being met? How did it affect your relationship?
3. What are your husbands interests and hobbies? How can you show more interest in them?
4. Do you feel that your home provides a sense of honor and fulfillment for your husband? Are there specific steps you can take to enhance the environment?
5. What are some areas in which you believe you excel as a partner, and where do you think you

could improve? How do you envision the ideal marriage, and what steps can you take to move closer to that vision?

CONNECT WITH GOD

Dear Father, thank You for the amazing way created husbands and wives to meet each other's needs. Help us to honor each other not only with our words but with our actions too. Give us the patience and strength to support each other when we stumble. Thank You, Holy Spirit, for being our constant Guide and Comforter. Teach us to love each other as You love us. In Jesus' name, Amen.

14 & 15

When You Are Building Alone & Four Principles for Building Alone

THE BIG IDEA

No matter where you are in your marriage today, you can confront any problem through complete submission to God, willingness to suffer, vision, and positive support.

REVIEW

Rebuilding a one-sided marriage requires dedication and faith. When you're the sole partner invested in nurturing the relationship, it can be a daunting journey. However, there are four biblical principles that offer guidance and hope, allowing you to work toward healing and restoration even when your spouse isn't actively participating. Regardless of your current marital situation, it's possible to confront and overcome challenges by aligning your efforts with God's wisdom. This approach empowers you to take control of your own actions and reactions, leading to positive change in your marriage.

1. Complete Submission

The foundation of rebuilding a one-sided marriage is complete submission to God. This is the most important issue that determines success or failure. It requires humbling yourself, recognizing your limitations, and acknowledging your dependence on God for guidance and strength. Pride and self-reliance can only lead to further destruction in your life and marriage. To find stability and safety, submit yourself fully to God. The safest place to be is under God's protective cover, and submission is the path to reach that sanctuary.

In difficult times, it's natural to want to defend yourself, especially when you've been hurt and rejected by your spouse. However, adopting a proud and defensive stance isn't the solution. Jesus teaches us to love our enemies, pray for those who mistreat us, bless those who curse us, and treat others as we wish to be treated.

The only way to conquer a negative spirit is with a positive one. Love overcomes hate, blessings overcome curses, and righteous behavior prevails over sin. Retaliating or reacting defensively to your spouse sets off a destructive cycle of sin-for-sin interactions. Unrighteous behavior never resolves problems, but righteous conduct does.

As you daily seek God for answers, as well as praying and petitioning Him about your problems, you not only will realize His faithfulness but will also experience the grace and peace that accompany humility.

2. Willingness to Suffer

Rebuilding a one-sided marriage requires the willingness to suffer. This doesn't mean damaging abuse but rather discomfort. Entrust yourself to God's care no matter what emotional, financial, spiritual, and domestic challenges may arise due to your spouse's actions.

Just as Jesus suffered for us, we must be prepared to endure hardships inflicted upon us without seeking retaliation or revenge and without succumbing to sin. We are called to follow Jesus' example by being righteous examples while entrusting ourselves to God.

When weighing the difficulties, consider the following:

- Leaving the marriage may alleviate suffering, but it often comes with its own emotional anguish, financial losses, and hardships, especially if children are involved.

- When you entered your marriage, you likely did not anticipate the problems you face now. Leaving your spouse does not guarantee a better outcome in a future relationship.
- Don't fall into the misconception that finding the "right" person ensures happiness. Every marriage encounters difficulties.

Jesus is the ultimate model for navigating challenging relationships. Follow His example and rely on Him for victory in adversity.

3. Vision for Your Marriage

What do you envision for your marriage's future? How would your spouse behave if they were righteous? Before achieving success, you must define what success means to you. Many marriages face challenges because they lack a clear plan and an understanding of God's will. The Bible serves as an invaluable source of vision. As you discover God's vision for your life and marriage, He will help you navigate rebuilding your relationship.

Pray, seek God's will, and read His Word. Ask God to give you vision and keep it at the forefront of your mind. Write it down and pray over it. In doing this, you aren't just living your life wandering around or trying to avoid problems. You are on a mission with a purpose, and you will succeed because God is with you.

4. Positive Support

During challenging times, we need someone to pray with us, encourage us, and hold us accountable to prevent us from making unwise decisions. Emotional and practical support is crucial, especially during the darkest hours of our lives.

The best place to look is a Bible-believing church. Look for a pastor, counselor, support group and/or godly individual to whom you can talk and with whom you can pray regularly concerning your situation. Be sure the counsel given you is biblical. You don't need a lot of opinions. You need godly counsel and encouragement.

Be careful with whom you share the details of your life and marriage. Find mature, godly individuals who can provide guidance and support. Don't be discouraged or influenced by unrighteous individuals who encourage you to do the wrong thing or persecute you for doing the right thing.

SCRIPTURE READING

> But he gives us more grace. That is why Scripture says:
>
> > "God opposes the proud
> >   but shows favor to the humble."

> Submit yourselves, then, to God. Resist the devil, and he will flee from you. Come near to God and he will come near to you (James 4:6–8).

> To this you were called, because Christ suffered for you, leaving you an example, that you should follow in his steps.
>
>> "He committed no sin,
>> and no deceit was found in his mouth."
>
> When they hurled their insults at him, he did not retaliate; when he suffered, he made no threats. Instead, he entrusted himself to him who judges justly. "He himself bore our sins" in his body on the cross, so that we might die to sins and live for righteousness; "by his wounds you have been healed" (1 Peter 2:21–24).

> When he, the Spirit of truth, comes, he will guide you into all the truth (John 16:13).

DISCUSSION QUESTIONS

1. Why is complete submission to God the first step when building alone? What makes this difficult?
2. What kinds of righteous suffering should a spouse be willing to endure? What would be going too far?
3. Why is having a clear "vision for your marriage" crucial when working toward its

restoration, and how can one discern God's vision for their relationship?

4. In what ways do wrong kinds of friends or advisors negatively impact marriages? What should you look for?

5. What happens when we try to overcome problems in our own strength rather than God's?

REFLECTION QUESTIONS

1. How willing are you to humble yourself and submit fully to God in your efforts to rebuild your marriage?

2. Do you tend to become defensive or retaliate when hurt or rejected by your spouse? How can you start responding with love and righteousness?

3. How can you distinguish between enduring discomfort for the sake of your relationship and accepting abusive behavior?

4. What vision do you have for the future of your marriage? How can your align your actions and efforts with this vision?

5. Have you identified a support system of mature and godly individuals who can pray with you, offer encouragement, and hold me accountable in your journey to restore your marriage?

CONNECT WITH GOD

Dear Father, there are times when I feel alone in working for our marriage. Help me not to despair but rather to submit completely to You. I am willing to count the cost and embrace the suffering that comes as I follow Your will. Give me the strength, joy, and peace I need to see this journey all the way to the finish line. Help me to remember that You are always with me. In Jesus' name, Amen.

16

Sweet and Sour Pleasure

THE BIG IDEA

With proper knowledge and preparation, the challenges of marriage can transform into rewarding experiences, and couples can avoid potential pitfalls.

REVIEW

If there is any one subject people need to be informed about, it is marriage. This relationship is a complex institution of spiritual, physical, financial, social, domestic, and mental requirements. It has the power to make men and women miserable or ecstatic, and they need correct information and serious preparation in order to make this lifelong commitment.

Today, many couples either don't know they should prepare themselves, or they don't know where to get help. It is a tragedy that even though we have so many educational programs for so many subjects, few of them teach people the skills necessary for marriage.

Couples need instruction in six important, "pleasure areas" of marriage: sex, communication, children, finances, in-laws, and blended family relationships. Before addressing each of these critical areas, though, it is essential to establish three principles for lasting marital success and pleasure. Jesus' "Parable of the Sower" highlights three qualities that hinder long-term success in both farming and life: stony ground, thorny ground, and shallow ground. If you find yourself represented by a certain type of bad soil, you can know that your relationship with Jesus and your spouse will not be as pleasurable or as successful as it should be. A fulfilling marriage requires us good soil that produces long-term fruitfulness.

Three Foundations for Permanent Success and Pleasure in Marriage

1. Knowledge: The Hard Soil

The first type of soil Jesus identifies as unproductive is the hard soil beside the road. The seeds sown on this hardened ground never to take root because they snatched away by birds. Whenever we enter into marriage without a soft heart seeking to know God's Word, we are sitting ducks for Satan's deception. Not only can he easily steal truth from a hardened heart, but he also can easily deceive the ignorant mind. God's Word provides practical guidance on children, sex, communication, finances, and family. Everything we need for success in life and marriage is waiting for us if we only will seek God first. Just as good soil becomes more receptive over time, our hearts should remain open to God's guidance throughout our lives.

2. Commitment: The Shallow Soil
The second type of soil that is incompatible with long-term fruitfulness is shallow soil. This kind of soil will accept a seed and allow it to grow for a period of time, but because the soil is so shallow, the seed cannot send roots down far enough to become stable and to find the moisture and nutrients it needs. When the sun begins to beat down upon the young plant, the soil cannot sustain it.

In marriage, vows to stand by each other "for better or worse, for richer or poorer, in sickness and in health" form the foundation a lifelong covenant. But in today's world, many people who get married are not totally committed. Every marriage is certain to have tough times. Although there is no glory in simply suffering through life, there is tremendous benefit in being faithful in bad times and learning from problems and failures.

There is great strength and security brought into a marriage when two people refuse to give up. Remember, a strong marriage is not produced from a fairy-tale existence—it comes from two people committed to working and sacrificing throughout their lives to make their marriage all it can be.

3. Discipline: The Thorny Soil
The third type of soil is the thorny soil that allows growth for a while, but the plant is eventually choked by competing vegetation. In our relationship with Jesus and our spouse, busyness and stress pose significant threats. We must be disciplined and true to our priorities. Many claim that God and family are their top priorities, but their actions often reveal a different reality. Time energy are both limited quantities, and thorny-soil individuals become consumed by everything except what truly matters.

Most of the things that ruin a marriage aren't bad things; rather, they are good things out of priority. To protect the pleasures of their marriage and make sure they will continue throughout their lives, both spouses must keep the soil clean and uncluttered. Have clear priorities and protect them.

SCRIPTURE READING

> My people are destroyed from lack of knowledge (Hosea 4:6).

Jesus answered, "It is written: 'Man shall not live on bread alone, but on every word that comes from the mouth of God'" (Matthew 4:4).

"So do not worry, saying, 'What shall we eat?' or 'What shall we drink?' or 'What shall we wear?' For the pagans run after all these things, and your heavenly Father knows that you need them. But seek first his kingdom and his righteousness, and all these things will be given to you as well. Therefore do not worry about tomorrow, for tomorrow will worry about itself. Each day has enough trouble of its own" (Matthew 6:31–34).

Jesus said, "If you hold to my teaching, you are really my disciples. Then you will know the truth, and the truth will set you free" (John 8:31–32).

DISCUSSION QUESTIONS

1. How can discovering conflicting expectations before marriage prevent problems later?
2. How can couples actively cultivate knowledge, commitment, and discipline in their relationship?
3. How can couples maintain open-heartedness and receptivity in their marriage, especially as time goes on?
4. What benefits come from enduring and persevering through marital struggles?

5. What are some common distractions that couples face, and how can they protect their marriage from being choked by these distractions?

RELECTION QUESTIONS

1. Do you view marriage as a relationship that has the potential to bring both happiness and challenges? How has your perception of marriage evolved over time?
2. In what areas of your life do you need to develop more discipline to support a healthy marriage?
3. How do your actions reflect your commitment to your spouse and your future together?
4. What steps can you take to ensure that your marriage doesn't fall into the trap of shallow soil?
5. What strategies can you use to avoid the distractions that could damage your relationship?

CONNECT WITH GOD

Dear Father, we praise You for the gift of marriage and the pleasures You intend it to bring. Forgive us where we have neglected to prepare and equip ourselves with Your wisdom. Soften our hearts to receive Your Word that guides us in every situation and increase our hunger to seek You first. May our marriage be fertile soil that produce love, hope, and joy. In Jesus' name, Amen.

17

Skills for Communication

THE BIG IDEA
Communication is the bridge that connects a husband and wife and gives them free access to each other's hearts and minds. Communication is not just important—it's essential.

REVIEW
Words possess the incredible power to wound or heal and to destroy or build up. We must discipline ourselves to use words that build up, strengthen, encourage, and heal. The opposite occurs when we succumb to the common temptation to wage warfare on our spouse because of frustrations or hurts. One day we will give an account to God for every single word we speak. If you have spoken words you know are wrong or harmful, you must repent to God and ask His forgiveness. You also need to repent to your spouse, children, and anyone else you may have hurt.

A husband and wife cannot become intimate as a couple without proper communication. Communication is the most important vehicle for our marriage relationships to establish oneness. Satan knows that if he can poison or prohibit our words, he can destroy our relationships. Commit yourself now to speak honest and loving words to your spouse daily to build and maintain a strong bridge of communication.

Proper communication in a marriage can occur only when the needs and differences of each spouse are understood and respected. There are five vital keys to communication in marriage.

1. Mutual Concern: Caring

We must be careful to show each other that we really care. This process begins as we affirm within ourselves the value and esteem we have for our spouses. It continues as we regularly tell them how important they are to us and how much we care about them. But the crowning glory of our demonstrations of how much we care comes from the overall communication of our lives.

Consider these seven daily components that convey concern:

1. Eye contact
2. Affection and body language

3. Countenance (the look on your face)
4. Voice level and tone
5. Frequency of contact and ease of emotional connection
6. Attitude toward serving and pleasing
7. Sensitivity to inner needs, hurts, and desires

Demonstrating these components in a positive, consistent manner lets your spouse know you care about them, making it easier for them to communicate with you. The absence of these components signals a lack of empathy and puts up a barrier. With every area of our hearts and lives, we must daily communicate to our spouses that we care about them.

Caring does not require strong emotions. The core of genuine, Christlike concern is to make a willful decision to appreciate and support another person. Feelings come and go, but care and empathy are core commitments. Once we have made this choice and acted it out in real ways, positive feelings almost always will follow.

2. Intellectual Devotion: Listening

There's a difference between hearing (a physiological function) and listening (an intellectual devotion). It is possible to hear something without really listening to it. It is like the old saying, "The lights are on, but no one is home." When your spouse speaks, listen carefully, as they may be communicating more than just words. If you don't listen, they will know it, and they will learn to save their words for someone who will listen.

Deal with distractions and problems regularly and promptly. Don't interrupt too often but ask questions on something you would like to have more information about or make brief comments appropriate to what is being said.

Maintain eye contact while listening as wandering eyes lead to wandering minds. Eyes are the windows to the soul and play a crucial role in effective communication. Once your spouse has finished saying something, giving a response is another essential way of communicating that you have tuned in to what has been said. Harsh, critical words or a blank, distant stare at the end of something freshly spoken quickly erects a wall between a couple who is trying to communicate.

3. Verbal Affirmation: Praise

Just as we approach God with thanksgiving and praise, we should extend gratitude and praise to our spouses. Praise is the key to unlocking a person's heart and nurturing love.

It's easy to forget our spouse's positive traits and focus on their flaws, leading to complaints and discontent. Discipline yourself to thank and praise your spouse, even for small things. By doing so, you pave the way for God to do great things in your marriage.

4. Loving Confrontation: Speaking the Truth in Love

Confrontation is inevitable in marriage, but it's essential to approach it with love and truth. Truth without love can be harsh, while love without truth lacks substance. Confrontation should begin with loving words of affirmation, emphasizing your commitment to your spouse.

Address concerns promptly to prevent them from accumulating and causing explosive conflicts later. Delaying discussions can allow negativity to fester and give room for the devil to sow discord.

When confronting your spouse, avoid assuming their thoughts or feelings. Refrain from blaming them for your emotions. Instead, strive for loving, truthful, and timely communication.

5. Intimate Discussion: Openness

The climax of marital communication is found in deeply personal, intimate conversation. Create a safe space where you and your spouse can share your innermost thoughts, feelings, and dreams. Use these intimate times to express your love and affection.

Do not take these special times for granted and do not hide your inner self from your spouse. The more you open up, the more you truly will know each other, and the deeper your intimacy and love for one another will be.

SCRIPTURE READING

> From the fruit of their mouth a person's stomach is filled;
> > with the harvest of their lips they are satisfied.
>
> The tongue has the power of life and death,
> > and those who love it will eat its fruit
> > (Proverbs 18:20–21).

But I tell you that everyone will have to give account on the day of judgment for every empty word they have spoken. For by your words you will be acquitted, and by your words you will be condemned (Matthew 12:36–37).

> Enter his gates with thanksgiving
> > and his courts with praise;
> > give thanks to him and praise his name
> > (Psalm 100:4).

Instead, speaking the truth in love, we will grow to become in every respect the mature body of him who is the head, that is, Christ (Ephesians 4:15).

> Never let loyalty and kindness leave you!
> > Tie them around your neck as a reminder.
> > Write them deep within your heart.

Then you will find favor with both God and people,
> and you will earn a good reputation
> (Proverbs 3:3–4 NLT).

DISCUSSION QUESTIONS

1. Why is communication the cornerstone of a successful marriage? How does it help two individuals connect on a deeper level?
2. What are some practical ways to ensure that words are used to uplift and strengthen rather than harm?
3. How are men and women different in their methods of communication?
4. How can being accountable for our words, both to God and to our spouse, contribute to a more positive and fruitful married life?
5. How do intimacy and openness deepen as spouses share more of themselves?

REFLECTION QUESTIONS

1. How do you view the role of communication in your own marriage? Is there room for improvement?
2. Have you ever experienced a situation where you needed to seek forgiveness from your spouse or loved ones for the words you've

spoken? How did that experience shape your understanding of accountability in communication?

3. What distractions do you need to eliminate to listen to your spouse better?
4. How do you currently demonstrate care and concern for your spouse in your daily interactions? What ways can you increase the demonstration of care and concern?
5. How can you balance truth with love during confrontations?

CONNECT WITH GOD

Dear Father, in Your wisdom You show us the power of words and the importance of communication in marriage. Please help us to balance love and truth as we honor our differences and respect our unique needs. Give us the strength to confront each other with kindness, offer praise freely, and engage in intimate, open conversations that deepen our connection. May the words of our mouths bless each other and honor You. In Jesus' name, Amen.

18

Skills for Financial Success

THE BIG IDEA
Money and material blessings can be a source of blessing and security when we follow the seven principles for financial prosperity God outlines in His Word.

REVIEW
Money and material blessings are meant by God to be a source of blessing and security, but for many couples, finances are a curse and a cause for fighting and insecurity in their relationships. Regardless of your financial situation, you need to respect the powerful influence finances have on your marriage.

The seven biblical principles for financial success are ownership, stewardship, leadership, contentment, faithfulness, freedom, and selflessness.

1. *Ownership*

Before we can truly succeed with our finances is, we must acknowledge that we own nothing and God owns everything. The first step on the road to financial freedom and security is to repent to God for taking possession of the things in our lives and refusing to recognize His ownership and authority over them. Then we must submit everything to Him and be obedient in all our financial decisions.

When we make decisions without praying or consulting the Word of God, the result is financial instability at best and often financial disaster somewhere down the line. God never promised us security or blessing apart from complete submission to Him. But when we surrender everything to God, there is no reason to fear because He will not allow His own belongings or decisions to be brought down.

According to Jesus' parable of the talents in Matthew chapter 25, the rewards are great when we accept our Master's money and do His will. But even though the world worships money, we must not. Rather, we should be stewards of our money as obedient servants of God. T Not only will we live in security and peace of mind, but we also will live in the prosperity and blessing God promises.

2. Stewardship

God directs us to test Him with our finances and let Him reveal His power and faithfulness by opening the windows of heaven and pouring out a blessing until it overflows. He also promises that He will rebuke the devourer for us if we give Him the first and best of our finances.

Tithing, which is giving the first tenth of our income to God, signifies our acknowledgment of His ownership of everything and demonstrates our faith in Him. Furthermore, tithing ensures the strength and functioning of the local church, which is the body of Christ on Earth. It also serves as a profound expression of gratitude to God for His blessings. God responds by bestowing more blessings upon us. It is important to note that the concept of giving money to God in order to get rich is not accurate. True prosperity means having more than enough to fulfill God's purpose for your life.

We should give out of love for God and appreciation for His blessings while also expecting to witness the results of His faithfulness in our finances.

3. Leadership

Planning and budgeting are crucial for avoiding financial problems. Without a solid direction, decisions are often based on personal whims and emotions. having a budget does not mean you should become legalistic with your finances. In fact, the process of developing a budget is as important as the budget itself. Once you have established a budget, you have a valuable tool to help you attain good money management skills.

Estate planning is another aspect of financial leadership. Every couple should seek counsel from a Christian lawyer, accountant, or estate planner to plan for the future. It is important to have up-to-date wills, proper amounts of life insurance and retirement funds, as well as a savings plan for education and other family needs. Open communication on these matters is vital to ensure that both spouses are well-informed and in agreement regarding their financial position.

4. Contentment

Contentment means being thankful for what we have and patiently awaiting God's provision and timing for more. Discontentment, on the other hand, drives us to chase after more and try to get it now. Advertisers are experts in inciting us to be discontented with what we have and to lure us to buy their products, even if we have to go into debt to do it. Many couples are in financial bondage today because they either are ungrateful for what they have or are trying to keep up with society.

Contentment means that we regularly give thanks to God for the blessings in our lives and are able to rest and be at peace with what we now have. We submit any desires for more with a thankful attitudes. The degree to which we cannot or will not submit our desires to God is the same degree to which our financial welfare is in danger. Money is a blessing, but it cannot replace God as our source of love, security, and happiness.

5. Faithfulness

Very few people ever get rich overnight. For the vast majority of us, faithfully working and wisely planning over many years will be how we establish financial security. Faithfulness is a foundational principle in God's design. We must discipline ourselves to make sound financial choices every day. Don't gamble on quick solutions to your desires or problems. Be faithful as you obey God's Word daily. Not only will you get what you are looking for, but when you get it, you will have it for the rest of your life.

6. Freedom

Debt is not a sin, but too much debt leads to bondage. If you are presently in debt, make a plan to get out and stick by it. As you pay off your existing debt, begin to save as much as you can in order that you can pay cash in the future for the things you need.

The Bible is very clear in stating that we are not to co-sign debts for others. This is wise advice from God for protection of our money and relationships. The Exceptions may include cosigning for your children to help them establish credit, but guidance and oversight are essential.

7. *Selflessness*

Selfishness poses a significant threat the well-being of any marriage. Lasting financial security and success begin with a mutual attitude of selflessness. Be willing to deny yourself and put your marriage and family's welfare first. This attitude reflects the character of Christ and invites God's blessings upon your marriage and finances.

SCRIPTURE READING

> The earth is the Lord's, and everything in it,
>   the world, and all who live in it;
> for he founded it on the seas
>   and established it on the waters
>   (Psalm 24:1–2).

"'Will a mere mortal rob God? Yet you rob me. But you ask, "How are we robbing you?" In tithes and offerings. You are under a curse—your whole nation—because you are robbing me. Bring the whole tithe into the storehouse, that there may be food in my house. Test me in this,' says the Lord

Almighty, 'and see if I will not throw open the floodgates of heaven and pour out so much blessing that there will not be room enough to store it. I will prevent pests from devouring your crops, and the vines in your fields will not drop their fruit before it is ripe,' says the LORD Almighty. 'Then all the nations will call you blessed, for yours will be a delightful land,' says the LORD Almighty" (Malachi 3:8–12).

But if we have food and clothing, we will be content with that. Those who want to get rich fall into temptation and a trap and into many foolish and harmful desires that plunge people into ruin and destruction. For the love of money is a root of all kinds of evil. Some people, eager for money, have wandered from the faith and pierced themselves with many griefs (1 Timothy 6:8–10).

DISCUSSION QUESTIONS

1. How does recognizing God's ultimate ownership impact our financial decisions and attitudes toward money?
2. In the context of marriage, how important is financial leadership and proper planning? How can couples work together in budgeting and financial decision-making?
3. How can we cultivate contentment in our lives, especially when society consistently pushes us to want more?

4. What are some practical steps couples can take to spend less than they earn? How does faithfulness in financial matters relate to other aspects of life?
5. How does selflessness contribute to financial harmony within a marriage?

REFLECTION QUESTIONS

1. Have you ever struggled with the concept of ownership in your financial decisions? How does the idea that everything belongs to God influence your perspective on money and possessions?
2. What is your thoughts and feelings about tithing? Have you ever tested God with your finances? If so, what were the results?
3. In what areas do you need to exercise better financial leadership and planning?
4. How can you practice selflessness in your financial decisions, especially related to your marriage and family?
5. How have daily financial choices and discipline contributed to your financial security?

CONNECT WITH GOD

Dear Father, You are our Provider. We recognize that everything we have is a gift from You, and we commit to stewarding Your resources faithfully. Help us to resist the temptation of greed and materialism and fill us with contentment for Your incredible blessings. Guide us to make wise financial decisions that reflect hearts of gratitude and trust. In every choice that we make, may we seek Your will and glorify You. In Jesus' name, Amen.

19

Skills for Successful Parenting

THE BIG IDEA

Next to our relationships with God and our spouses, our children should be the most important priorities in our lives. They are precious gifts that require and deserve our time, love, and attention.

REVIEW

When we give our children the necessary time, love, and attention, we invest wisely. They bless our lives and grow to be responsible adults of whom we can be proud. But when we fail to love our children and to meet their needs properly, they can become major problems and a threat to our marriages.

Every child has four major needs that only God can completely satisfy. These needs are identity, security, purpose, and acceptance. As adults, we are able to establish a personal relationship with Jesus and our spouses in order to find the deep, inner satisfaction that we need. Although our children can accept Christ and love Him at a young age, during the first 18 years of their lives, having their needs met is largely dependent upon us.

The goal should be to wean our children from our care and usher them into the arms of God. That is our real purpose as parents. Children's understanding of who God is and what He is like is most influenced by the character of their parents and the parents' treatment of the children. When parents demonstrate a balance of love and truth and invest themselves faithfully in the development of their child, it will be easy for that child to understand and accept the Lord. But when a parent is absent, rejecting, cruel, abusive and/or weak, the child will not have their needs met and will have a more difficult time understanding and accepting God.

As parents, our twofold purpose is to

1. usher the child into an understanding and acceptance of Jesus Christ as Lord and Savior, and
2. meet the four basic needs of the child.

When a child is grown and ready to leave home, the parents should be able to say two things: "We have done everything we could to reveal the love and nature of God to our child and to lead him or her to Jesus," and "We have met every major need in our child's life in a faithful and sacrificial manner."

The best thing we can do is love God and live a life that is pleasing to Him. Children are much more influenced by who we are and what we do than by what we say or teach. Parents who live what they believe to the best of their abilities are doing the best possible thing to train their child or children properly.

How to Meet the Four Major Needs of a Child

1. Acceptance
From the moment a child is born, they begin to sense the nature of their environment. In order for a child to feel safe and secure, parents must demonstrate love and acceptance through four major ways:

- **Physical Affection:** Regardless of age, children need physical touch and affection from both parents. The less parents touch and hold their children, the more emotionally detached and rejected they are likely to feel. Regular, warm displays of physical affection convey acceptance powerfully.
- **Verbal Affirmation:** Praise and compliments are crucial for a child's development, and they

need to hear "I love you" from their parents daily. Criticism or silence signal a lack of acceptance. Parents must never shame or bully their children.
- **Availability:** While quality time is essential, children also need quantity time. Parents who spend too much time away from their children leave them feeling alone and unimportant. Children spell love T-I-M-E.
- **Expression:** Children need to a sense of belonging and a sense of identity and individual expression. While parents should teach obedience and uphold certain standards, they should not overwhelm their children's individual identities with their own opinions or dominant personalities.

2. Identity

Every person needs to feel unique and significant. Parents play a vital role in nurturing this sense of identity by telling their children how special they are. Comparing children or pressuring them to conform to the family system can hinder their self-expression. While boundaries must be established, children should be allowed to express themselves within the framework of love and order.

3. Security
Children's sense of security largely comes from the stability of their parents' lives. Conflict at home or financial stress can make a child feel insecure, even if these issues are not openly discussed. Parents should respect their children's emotional vulnerability and strive to create an atmosphere of stability and love. Children need rules and boundaries. And they need to be lovingly disciplined and held accountable when they disobey and rebel. Children feel loved and secure when they are raised with a balance of accountability and acceptance.

4. Purpose
Even at a young age, children should be taught that God has a unique purpose for their lives. Parents can convey this by affirming their child's uniqueness and telling them that God created them for a special purpose that will be revealed one day

Parents meet their children's need for purpose by giving them household and family responsibilities. As children grow, parents should gradually increase these responsibilities while ensuring a balance with fun and serving in church and the community. No person will ever feel fulfilled or have a true purpose in life until they fulfill God's call on their life.

There Is No Excuse for Abuse
When it comes to child discipline and spanking, four critical issues must be considered:

1. Abusing a Child Is Without Excuse
Abuse subjects a child to harmful physical, emotional, or spiritual influences. Proper spanking, however, does not damage a child but rather reveals the truth that there are consequences for poor behavior. It also underscores the concept that God punishes disobedience. Hitting a child randomly all over their body with your hand or an instrument is unsafe and unhealthy. Yelling at a child, calling them names, disciplining them in public, and lying to instill fear in them damages a child emotionally.

2. The Anti-Spanking Lobby
The philosophy against spanking contradicts God's Word and lacks consistency. Humanism teaches that children do not have a sign nature, but the truth is every person will self-destruct without proper discipline and restraint. Children are naturally sinful, and they must be taught to obey. Correct discipline teaches a child to respect others and to restrain his or her behavior.

3. Spanking Is Right but Not the Answer in Every Situation

Not all disciplinary situations require spanking. Parents should be sensitive to their child's emotional needs and consider alternative forms of discipline when appropriate. Discipline should not damage the child but should serve as a means to get their attention and encourage better behavior.

4. Parents Must Be in Agreement

It is crucial for parents to agree on disciplinary methods and support each other. Conflict over discipline can harm children and marriages. Both parents should be involved in discipline decisions, and disagreements should be discussed privately to maintain unity.

Raising children is a divine responsibility. Through love, nurturing, and proper discipline, parents can guide their children toward a meaningful relationship with God and help them become responsible and fulfilled adults.

SCRIPTURE READING

> Children are a heritage from the Lord,
> > offspring a reward from him.
> Like arrows in the hands of a warrior
> > are children born in one's youth.
> Blessed is the man
> > whose quiver is full of them.

> They will not be put to shame
> > when they contend with their opponents
> > in court (Psalm 127:3–5).
>
> Start children off on the way they should go,
> > and even when they are old they will not
> > turn from it (Proverbs 22:6).
>
> Do not withhold discipline from a child;
> > if you punish them with the rod, they will
> > not die (Proverbs 23:13).

Children, obey your parents in the Lord, for this is right. "Honor your father and mother"—which is the first commandment with a promise—"so that it may go well with you and that you may enjoy long life on the earth." Fathers, do not exasperate your children; instead, bring them up in the training and instruction of the Lord (Ephesians 6:1–4).

DISCUSSION QUESTIONS

1. If raising children is a sacred duty bestowed by God, then what role should faith play in our approach to parenting?
2. How can parents meet the four basic needs of their children while balancing love and discipline?
3. In what ways do parents' behaviors and beliefs shape their children's understanding of God?

4. How can parents provide a sense of security and purpose in their children's lives?
5. How can parents ensure that they are in agreement when it comes to disciplinary methods and parenting decisions? What are the potential consequences when parents are not on the same page in raising their children?

REFLECTION QUESTIONS

1. How have your upbringing and belief system influenced your perspective on parenting?
2. Are you meeting your child's needs for acceptance, identity, security, and purpose? Which areas need more focus?
3. What responsibilities are appropriate for each of your children, given their ages and maturity levels?
4. Are you sensitive to your children's unique personalities and callings from God? Or are you forcing your desires on them?
5. Does your relationship with your spouse modeling God's love? How does it impact your children?

CONNECT WITH GOD

Dear Father, You have given us the sacred responsibility and privilege of raising our children to know and love You. We want to steward them well for Your glory. Give us wisdom every day as we meet their needs for acceptance, identity, security, and purpose. Help us to model Your Son in our words, actions, and attitudes. May our children come to know and love you for the rest of their lives.. In Jesus' name, Amen.

20

Skills for Sexual Pleasure

THE BIG IDEA

To understand the nature and importance of sexual intimacy, we first must remember that it was God who created this delight in the first place. For this reason, God has told us in His Word how we can fulfill our need for sex while avoiding the sensual destruction everywhere around us.

REVIEW

Sexual intimacy is a powerful force that brings men and women together, offering both pleasure and the potential for procreation. Sex is the universally spoken language of love, but it has also been one of humanity's most exploited weaknesses. God designed sex to bring us pleasure and to create a deep bond through intimacy and mutual satisfaction. As with all of God's creation, Satan tries to pervert sex and use it to destroy us. God tells us in His Word how we can fulfill our need for sex while avoiding the sensual destruction everywhere around us.

There are six sexual practices that God forbids:

1. Sex outside of marriage (adultery and fornication)
2. Sex with a member of the same sex (homosexuality)
3. Sex with a family member (incest)
4. Sex with minors (pedophilia)
5. Sex with animals (bestiality)
6. Sexual fantasies or desires for someone other than your spouse (adultery in God's eyes; includes all forms of pornography and lustful fantasies)

Within God's parameters, couples are free to enjoy sex together. God is not a prude, and sex is not dirty. It's a wonderful creation designed to give us pleasure. Instead of trying to keep something good from us, God is trying to protect us from harm. By trusting in God's wisdom and adhering to His guidelines, couples can enthusiastically pursue sexual fun and fulfillment in marriage.

When considering sexual practices not explicitly addressed in Scripture, it's helpful to ask some important questions:

1. Does this increase oneness and intimacy?
2. Is it mutually pleasurable or at least mutually agreed upon? (Spouses should not be forced to do anything against their wills.)
3. Is it hygienically and physically safe?
4. Can I do this with a clear conscience before God. (If we cannot do something by faith, it is sin.)
5. Is this something I would want my children to practice in their marriages someday?

If a sexual practice passes these criteria, there should be no hesitation in enjoying it within the confines of marriage. However, if it fails to meet these standards, it's advisable to pray and seek guidance or simply decide not to do it. The most important aspect of sex is not what it does for you personally but what it does for you both as a couple before God.

Men typically have a stronger appetite for sex and a need to fulfill this urge in marriage, but they also have some major problems. The first is misinformation and deception. Pornography presents a distorted and unhealthy portrayal of sex. Men who consume pornography are influenced by these unrealistic depictions, which can lead to selfish and destructive behavior within their marriages.

Men, if you are involved in pornography, get out! It will destroy your life and your marriage. Stop and turn your heart to God. honestly share your sexual needs with your wife and express your desire to please her. Let her do what she is comfortable doing, as you aggressively serve her and seek to fulfill her needs. If you will, you will find lasting fulfillment in a practice that brings a lifetime of pleasure, not pain.

Another challenge that men face is ignorance of a women's sexual makeup. Men often think that women are just like them, so they expect their wives to turn on and off as quickly as they do and have "mountaintop" experiences every time. But women are very different from men when it comes to sex, both physically and emotionally. Men need to recognize and respect these differences, showing care and nonsexual affection toward their wives throughout the day. They should maintain good hygiene and grooming habits, prioritize foreplay, and consistently compliment their wives' beauty, both inside and out.

Just as a man should meet his wife's need for love and romance, a woman should meet her husband's visual and physical needs. A wife needs to reveal her body to her husband to allow full, satisfying body contact as a part of sex. For a man, sex is not just a preference or a pleasant event—it is a major need in his life.

Women also face significant issues when it comes to their sexual lives. The first is previous sexual and/or physical abuse. Many women have experienced sexual abuse by family members, friends, or strangers, and they react in different ways. Some may engage in promiscuous behavior to cope with feelings of guilt and dirtiness, while others become frigid and sexually unresponsive. Other women refuse to deal with the pain of their past, but they cannot function normally in the present. Addressing and healing from past abuse is essential for a woman's personal well-being and a healthy marital relationship.

The second challenge women encounter is guilt related to past sexual experiences, such as premarital sex, abortion, or affairs. Forgiveness is available through repentance and faith in Christ's sacrifice. Women should confess their sins to God, turn away from them, and accept that they are forgiven, allowing them to fully enjoy their sexual relationship with their spouse.

SCRIPTURE READING

> Then the LORD God made a woman from the rib he had taken out of the man, and he brought her to the man.
>
> The man said,
>
> > "This is now bone of my bones
> > and flesh of my flesh;

> she shall be called 'woman,'
>> for she was taken out of man."

That is why a man leaves his father and mother and is united to his wife, and they become one flesh (Genesis 2:22–24).

The husband should fulfill his marital duty to his wife, and likewise the wife to her husband. The wife does not have authority over her own body but yields it to her husband. In the same way, the husband does not have authority over his own body but yields it to his wife. Do not deprive each other except perhaps by mutual consent and for a time, so that you may devote yourselves to prayer. Then come together again so that Satan will not tempt you because of your lack of self-control (1 Corinthians 7:3–5).

Marriage should be honored by all, and the marriage bed kept pure, for God will judge the adulterer and all the sexually immoral (Hebrews 13:4).

DISCUSSION QUESTIONS

1. In what ways does modern society influence our perceptions and practices of sexual intimacy?
2. How does your faith shape your attitude toward sex within a marriage?
3. How important is mutual pleasure and consent in a marital sexual relationship?

4. How can couples effectively communicate their different sexual needs and desires while maintaining respect and love?
5. How should couples handle issues related to past sexual abuse in the context of their marriage?

REFLECTION QUESTIONS
1. What are your personal beliefs and boundaries regarding sexual practices in marriage?
2. How have external influences like tv, movies, and social media shaped your expectations of sex in marriage?
3. Have you and your spouse discussed your sexual desires, boundaries, and any concerns you may have? If not, how might you initiate such a conversation?
4. How well do you understand your partner's sexual needs, and what steps could you take to improve this understanding?
5. How do you cope with any personal guilt or shame related to past sexual experiences, and what steps can you take to overcome these feelings?

CONNECT WITH GOD

Dear Father, You created sex to be a wonderful gift for husbands and wives. Purify our hearts and minds as we reject the world's lies in favor of Your unwavering truth. Help us to meet each other's needs with grace and selflessness. Please forgive us for the times we have failed to honor You with this sacred gift. We submit every aspect of our marriage to You. In Jesus' name, Amen.

21

Skills for In-Law Relations

THE BIG IDEA
When two individuals get married, their families are linked together in a common bond that has a tremendous potential for blessing if properly stewarded.

REVIEW
One of the great blessings of marriage is the opportunity to extend your family. Through marriage, not only two individuals, but also two families are linked together in a common bond. This special aspect of the marital union has tremendous potential for blessing our lives whenever we understand and are proper stewards over this expanded family relationship. However, when in-law and extended family relations are misunderstood or mishandled, few mistakes have greater potential to devastate a marriage.

There are four fundamental principles to navigating relationships between spouses, parents, and in-laws.

1. *The Principle of Honor*

Many married couples don't understand the difference between authority and honor. God's Word says we should always honor our parents. When we are living in their home, we also are under their authority, and we should obey them and treat them with respect. Once we get married, we should still treat our parents with honor and respect, but they no longer have authority over us.

One of the most devastating problems in a marriage is for a parent or in-law to dominate or unduly influence the couple. Sometimes they do this by intimidating personalities, and other times, a parent will manipulate with guilt or money to control their married adult children and to gain influence with them. This emasculates the man because it takes away his honor and significance.

Each husband and wife must understand the legitimate violation their spouses will experience if one of their parents is allowed to transgress the proper boundaries in their home and marriage. When you get married, you must sever the ties of authority your parents have in your life. This doesn't mean you cannot take their advice or even seek their counsel. Rather, you are not obligated to do so or to follow their advice. Of course, this does not mean you should ever dishonor your parents or in-laws. When you stand up to them and resist or correct something they are doing, always treat them with dignity and love.

2. The Principle of Separation

When we get married, we must reprioritize our relationships with our parents. They can no longer occupy the top position on our lists of priorities. For the sake of our marriages, we must make our spouses our first relationship commitment and top priority. For this reprioritizing to take place properly, we must have a healthy separation from our parents and in-laws and be able to spend quality and quantity time with our spouses and children, alone. When we are able to separate properly from our parents, we are able to establish our own identities. We are also able to bond together as a married couple and as a family. People not willing to separate properly from their parents should not get married.

Carefully consider the following four questions:

1. Do you or your spouse feel violated by the frequent presence or strong influence of your parents or in-laws?
2. Do you or your spouse spend a large amount of your free time talking to, or being with, your

parents, in-laws, or extended family, including brothers, sisters, cousins, and so forth?

3. Are most of your activities and close relationships with parents, in-laws, or extended family?
4. Do you find it hard to make major personal or marital decisions without the approval of your parents, in-laws, or extended family?

If you answered yes to any of these four questions, you really need to think seriously about what you are doing. If you answered yes to two or more questions, you need to take some immediate action for the sake of your marriage. Although it may be difficult at first to make a change everyone concerned will be better off in the long run if you take action now. Your parents and in-laws will respect you much more if you lovingly establish and maintain healthy parameters in your relationship with them.

Many mothers-in-law are a tremendous blessing to their married children and grandchildren, as are many fathers-in-law. However, some women have a more difficult time allowing their children to separate from them. When this happens, a problem relationship is sure to develop. There are three elements that normally create a problem mother-in-law situation:

1. The mother-in-law lacks other fulfilling relationships.

2. The mother-in-law's identity is wrapped up with her child.
3. The mother-in-law is adversarial with her child's spouse.

A parent's use of a child to prop themselves up emotionally is called "triangling." Rather than God and the spouse providing necessary emotional strength, a parent turns to a child (or children) for emotional security. There are multiple problems with using a child to gain the fulfillment in life that a parent should seek elsewhere. First, it's abusive to the child because it prevents the child from developing properly. Second, it perpetuates problems in the parents' lives and prevents both the parents and the children from leading normal lives. Triangling breaks the child but won't fix the parent. Third, when a parent emotionally attaches to a child of the opposite sex, cross-gender identification occurs. Boys learn to be masculine from their fathers, while girls learn to be feminine from their mothers. Big problems happen when a parent does not attach to the same-sex child or if a parent overly attaches to a child of the opposite sex. Finally, triangling can lead parents to over-attach to their children, causing devastation and insecurity when the child grows up and leaves home.

A problematic mother-in-law needs to be told that she should pursue fulfillment with God, her husband, and/or other areas of life. Although she needs to know her child loves her, that child cannot be her sole focus.

3. The Principle of Protection

In marriage, both spouses must commit to protecting each other from the interference or criticism of their respective parents. Avoid criticizing your spouse to your parents, and do not allow your parents to criticize your spouse to you. When parents begin to meddle in your relationship, address the issue lovingly but firmly.

When both partners protect each other from parental interference or criticism, it builds an atmosphere of safety and trust within the relationship. Failure to do so can lead to significant damage. It is crucial to honor your spouse and insist on the same level of respect from your parents and family.

When adult children appropriately assert themselves in these situations, it often results in a positive environment of respect that enhances the relationship with their parents moving forward. In rare cases where parents refuse to respect these wishes, an adult child must prioritize their spouse and marriage, even if it means severing ties with the parents.

This same principle of protection also applies in your parents' relationships with your children. Your parents' time with your children is a privilege, not a right. So, when they expose your child to influences of which you disapprove, they need to be confronted.

If they refuse to respect your wishes, do not let your children be around them without your direct supervision. As a parent, you must not be intimidated, for your children are God's precious and valuable gifts. Whoever they are left with should be someone who respects and supports your values.

4. The Principle of Friendship

View your parents as precious friends in your life who have made a lifelong commitment to you. Prioritize spending regular time with them to keep your friendship fresh and alive. Handle situations as you would with any good friends if they happen to cross boundaries in your home or marriage. This approach keeps the relationship healthy and respectful and also serves as a preventive measure against potential issues.

Unless you know God has told you to do it, it's generally considered unwise to live with in-laws. The exception is in the case of their old age or failing health. We owe it to our parents to help them and care for them in their golden years or during times of distress. Although these circumstances do not always mean they should live with you, when parents are in need of care because of sickness or old age, you should do everything possible to assist them.

SCRIPTURE READING

That is why a man leaves his father and mother and is united to his wife, and they become one flesh (Genesis 2:24).

> Children's children are a crown to the aged,
> and parents are the pride of their children
> (Proverbs 17:6).

But if a widow has children or grandchildren, these should learn first of all to put their religion into practice by caring for their own family and so repaying their parents and grandparents, for this is pleasing to God (1 Timothy 5:4).

DISCUSSION QUESTIONS

1. How can extended family positively or negatively influence a marriage?
2. In what ways can couples honor their parents while also establishing healthy boundaries and maintaining their independence within the marriage?
3. How can favoritism shown by parents or grandparents be addressed in a family setting?
4. How can couples discern between helpful advice and interference from parents?
5. How can maintaining a friendship with parents benefit both the marriage and the

extended family? What are some practical ways to cultivate and nurture this friendship while respecting boundaries?

REFLECTION QUESTIONS

1. How do you view the role of your parents and in-laws in your marriage? Do you see them more as authority figures, friends, or a combination of both?
2. How have you established independence from your parents since getting married? What challenges have you faced?
3. Do you believe you have struck a healthy balance between spending time with your spouse and maintaining relationships with extended family members? Are there any adjustments you would like to make in this regard?
4. Have you ever found yourself in a situation where a parent or family member criticized your spouse or interfered in your relationship? How did you handle it, and what lessons did you learn from that experience?
5. Think about your relationship with your own parents and in-laws. How can you cultivate a sense of friendship and mutual respect while also maintaining boundaries in your interactions with them?

CONNECT WITH GOD

Dear Father, thank You for the gift of extended family. Help us to honor our parents and in-laws while keeping You and our spouses as our first priorities. Give us the wisdom we need to navigate challenging moments with honor and grace. May we approach each situation with a spirit of love and understanding, reflecting Your love in all our interactions. Please bless our families today. In Jesus' name, Amen.

22

Skills for Remarriage and Blended Families

THE BIG IDEA
You can succeed in remarriage or a blended family if you look to God and follow His directions.

REVIEW
Navigating the complexities of remarriage and blended families can be an arduous journey. But as Christians, we find solace in the belief that God offers guidance if we seek Him and follow His path.

Blended families comprise about half of the families in the United States. The challenge for remarriages and blended families is that they have a higher rate of divorce than first marriages, and face even more difficult issues. However, you can succeed in a remarriage or blended family.

In the aftermath of a painful divorce, many people make "inner vows" or promises to themselves as a way to cope. These inner vows are often rooted in bitterness and judgment, serving as self-protective mechanisms to prevent similar pain from happening again in the future. The problem with inner vows is that they are self-directed promises that demonstrate an attitude of not trusting God and allowing Him to lead us. When we respond to situations in life by boldly swearing what we will and will not do, it makes us God. It's a form of arrogance and rebellion. And that's why it's wrong and of the devil.

Another danger of inner vows is they are always exacted from the people in our present and future. When you say to yourself, "No one's ever going to treat me like that again!" you are actually speaking about your future spouse. And, though your anger is at your ex-spouse, the price will be exacted from someone who is innocent. Unless you have forgiven your ex-spouse and those in your past who have significantly harmed you, you will carry the pain and problems into your future.

Forgiveness is the cornerstone of emotional healing and self-love. When you forgive, you release the emotional and practical debt that others owe you, just as God does when He forgives you. Forgiveness means refraining from seeking revenge or punishing others for their mistakes. It involves letting go and moving on.

This includes forgiving yourself for any mistakes you have made in the past. Remember that your capacity to extend grace to others is closely tied to your ability to receive God's forgiveness and grace for your own errors. You cannot give away what you do not possess. Forgiveness is the key to breaking free from your past and fostering a healthy future.

Once you've addressed the issues of your past, you're able to focus on your present marriage. And in every marriage, there are important decisions to be made that determine its success.

Will You Commit?

The danger of remarriage is that you can come into it with lower trust and higher expectations. Therefore, you must do everything possible to raise your level of trust and have realistic expectations. The purpose of dating is to examine the character of another person and your level of compatibility. If you remarry "on the rebound," or without the proper dating process, you're likely to marry a person you are still sizing up. If you do not know whether this is the person to whom you want to commit, you will be set up for failure.

Regardless of the pain and mistakes of the past, plant your feet in the present. Commit to this marriage. Without commitment, you will enter a vicious cycle of destructive behavior. Every time a problem exists, you'll wonder if it's what will break up your marriage. Because you think that way, you are not able to give everything to the relationship—and because you are cautious and uncommitted, your spouse will begin to withhold as well. In the end, your fears will come true, so you will end that marriage and go on to the next. That's the very reason statistics say a person's chances of divorce rise every time he or she remarries. You, however, can stop this from coming true in your life simply by making a firm decision to commit to your marriage.

Will You Be "One"?

God designed marriage to operate as a complete joining and sharing of two lives. The intimacy and union of marriage is so profound that God used the word "one" to describe it. Things become one by melding together. In marriage, everything that was owned or administrated separately is now surrendered to the co-ownership and control of the relationship. Consequently, anything you refuse to surrender to your spouse for his or her input and influence will damage your relationship and create deep resentment.

If you have children from a previous marriage, then you must give your children to your new spouse. You cannot withhold them. Likewise, if your spouse has children from a previous marriage, then you must receive full ownership of those children.

If you think you're doing your children a favor by withholding them from your marriage to protect them, you're wrong. It only perpetuates insecurity within them as it allows them to divide you from your spouse and sabotage your new marriage. This is where you need to lose the word "my" and adopt the word "ours"—whether it's with children, money, or anything else.

Of course, you must remain sensitive to the emotions of the children and the particulars of your situation. It's usually better for a blended family if the biological parent enforces the discipline on his or her children. This is especially true when the marriage is new and the relationship between your children and your new spouse is still developing. But even then, your spouse must have input into the parameters of discipline and the overall disposition of the children. You must be a team and be influenced by each other.

Your spouse may not love your children like you do because of your biological bond, but they can still love your children in a great way In fact, the greatest form of love is what the Bible calls *agape*, and it's the love that Jesus demonstrated for us when He died for us on the cross. The form of love does not depend upon emotions; rather, it's an act of the will.

Will You Embrace the Good as Well as the Bad?

Child support, negative influence on the children by an ex-spouse, responsibility to care for biological or nonbiological children during times of visitation, and so on can be touchy issues. But husbands and wives who remarry must understand that they're taking on all the good—and the bad—from each other's lives. You don't keep the good and throw out the bad. When you go through difficult times, you don't separate—you draw even closer.

Every family should be built around a marriage. A family built around children, or anything else, would be like an atom without a nucleus. Without a nucleus, the atomic particles—the protons, neutrons, and electrons—have nothing to orbit around. In the same way, a blended family cannot be stable without a stable marriage at its core.

Some remarried couples have this mindset: "If this marriage doesn't last, I don't want my children to resent me for the rest of my life for choosing my spouse over them. So, I'll consider the possibility of divorce in this decision as I prefer my children over my spouse." Don't let fear create a downward spiral of bad decisions, leading to bad feelings in the marriage, leading to your worst fears coming true. If you see yourself on this downward cycle, stop letting fear control you. Take control of your thoughts and let common sense and wisdom lead you.

Remember that your children need to witness a healthy marriage as an example for their future relationships. Show through your actions, words, and attitudes that your marriage is a priority, without making your children feel rejected or resentful toward your spouse.

Feelings toward an ex-spouse can sometimes linger and even overshadow the emotions for a current spouse. It is important to remember that the highest form of love is a decision, not an emotion. Choose to focus on your current spouse and allow your decisions to shape your emotions, rather than the other way around.

Negative influence from an ex-spouse on your children and family can be heart-wrenching. Stand strong in truth and love, believing in the power of these forces to overcome lies and hate. Maintain open lines of communication and avoid using your children as intermediaries. Deal directly and respectfully with your ex-spouse, and if you meet face to face, make sure another person is present with you.

Blended families require heightened standards to minimize potential issues. Modesty must be maintained in a manner that is consistent with common sense and propriety. Immodesty leads to a higher level of sexual temptation. Nonbiological family members of the opposite sex should not spend time alone in an inappropriate manner. Many times when children are being sexually abused, they will go to their biological parent and tell them something is wrong. This should not be dismissed. Sexual abuse by a stepparent or a stepsibling must be dealt with in a direct and serious manner.

Helping your children adjust to a new stepparent involves addressing their feelings about the past, forgiving any wrongs, and assuring them that the presence of a new partner is not the reason for not reconciling with their other parent. Introduce your new partner gradually and involve your children in the process. Focus on building a foundation of trust and understanding within your blended family.

SCRIPTURE READING

"Again, you have heard that it was said to the people long ago, 'Do not break your oath, but fulfill to the Lord the vows you have made.' But I tell you, do not swear an oath at all: either by heaven, for it is God's throne; or by the earth, for it is his footstool; or by Jerusalem, for it is the city of the Great King. And do not swear by your head, for you cannot make even one hair white or black. All you need to say is simply 'Yes' or 'No'; anything beyond this comes from the evil one" (Matthew 5:33–37).

"For if you forgive other people when they sin against you, your heavenly Father will also forgive you. But if you do not forgive others their sins, your Father will not forgive your sins" (Matthew 6:14–15).

If we claim to be without sin, we deceive ourselves and the truth is not in us. If we confess our sins, he is faithful and just and will forgive us our sins and purify us from all unrighteousness. If we claim we have not sinned, we make him out to be a liar and his word is not in us. My dear children, I write this to you so that you will not sin. But if anybody does sin, we have an advocate with the Father—Jesus Christ, the Righteous One. He is the atoning sacrifice for our sins, and not only for ours but also for the sins of the whole world (1 John 1:8–2:2).

DISCUSSION QUESTIONS

1. How do inner vows impact the dynamics of remarriage and blended families, and what are the potential consequences of holding onto these vows?
2. What role does forgiveness play in the success of a remarriage and a blended family?
3. How can remarried couples prioritize their relationship while ensuring their children feel loved and secure?

4. What are some practical strategies for introducing a new romantic partner to children in a way that builds trust and minimizes resistance or discomfort?
5. How can a blended family maintain a healthy balance between respecting the past and embracing the present and future?

REFLECTION QUESTIONS

1. Have you made any inner vows as a result of past hurts, and how might they be affecting your current relationships?
2. How have you dealt with forgiveness in the context of past relationships and in your current family dynamic?
3. How do you manage financial obligations and influences from past relationships within your current family?
4. What is your strategy for including and valuing children from previous marriages in your blended family?
5. What boundaries and standards have you established in your blended family to ensure propriety and respect?

CONNECT WITH GOD

Father God, You are the God who redeems and renews. We submit our marriage and family to You. Help us to forgive past hurts and release inner vows as we move forward in freedom. Heal our hearts and give us the courage to commit fully to our spouses, to treat each other's children as our own, and to prioritize our marriage as the foundation of our blended family. May our homes reflect Your love, and may our families be a testament to Your redeeming power. In Jesus' name, Amen.

Notes

4. The Law of Pursuit

1. James Strong, Hebrew-Chaldee Dictionary, *Strong's Exhaustive Concordance of the Bible* (Iowa Falls, IA: Riverside Book and Bible House, 1986), Hebrew #1692.
2. Ibid., Greek #26.

Printed in the USA
CPSIA information can be obtained
at www.ICGtesting.com
JSHW012108020824
67483JS00004B/34

9 781960 870223